Political
Participation
in Canada:
Prospects for
Democratic
Citizenship

William Mishler

Canadian Controversies Series

Macmillan of Canada

Canadian Cataloguing in Publication Data

Mishler, William, 1947 –
   Political participation in Canada

(Canadian controversies series)

Includes index.
ISBN 0 – 7705 – 1770 – 6 pa.

1. Political participation – Canada. I. Title. II. Series.

JL196.M58   329   C79 – 094416 – 2

Printed in Canada for
The Macmillan Company of Canada Limited
70 Bond Street
Toronto, Ontario
M5B 1X3

Contents

Canadian Controversies Series

Canadian political commentators have adopted the full range of political styles, from cold detachment to partisan advocacy. The Canadian Controversies Series is disciplined by the idea that while political analysis must be based on sound descriptive and explanatory modes of thought, social scientists should not abnegate the role of evaluating political systems. Such evaluations require a conscious approach to the inter-relationships between facts and values, empirical and normative considerations in politics.

Each theme in the series has been chosen to illustrate some basic principles of Canadian political life and to allow the respective authors freedom to develop normative positions on the related problems. It is hoped that the volumes will stimulate debate and advance public understanding of some of the major questions which confront the Canadian political system. By treating the enduring themes and problems in Canada, the authors will also illustrate the important contribution that social science can offer to politics in terms of facts, ideas, theories, and comparative frameworks within which meaningful controversy can take place. Creative political thought must not be divorced from the political fabric of a country but form an integral part of it.

ROBERT J. JACKSON
General Editor

Preface

Political theory, it has been said, is a "mixture of description, neutral generalization, and moral principle". Nowhere is this more evident, but less appreciated, than in the central and continuing debate in democratic theory over the role of citizen participation in the political process. Intertwined in a complex and often confusing literature are normative questions (such as whether participation is a legitimate or sufficient source of political authority, how much participation is desirable, and who should be permitted to participate) together with empirical questions (such as who does participate, how extensively, in what political activities, under what conditions, and with what consequences for society and the individual). Unfortunately, not only are the answers that have been provided to these questions often contradictory, but many of the most important questions have never been systematically addressed.

A primary reason that the debate in democratic theory has not been more productive has been the tendency of social scientists to treat analysis and evaluation as separate, if not antagonistic, concerns. Although appeals for a synthesis of facts and values are commonplace, few attempts to integrate the two have succeeded. Nor have we permitted ourselves to speculate creatively about the important social questions whose boundaries extend beyond normative and empirical considerations and encroach upon the hypothetical. What if citizens did behave rationally? What if they were better informed and were tolerant of the rights of others? What if they were to become more interested in politics and began to participate in activities other than voting? What if they were provided greater opportunites for effective participation in the family, at school, and in the workplace, as well as in the political process; what would be the consequences for society and the implications for democratic theory?

Because such questions traditionally have not been considered adaptable to empirical modes of inquiry, social scientists have tended to avoid social prescription, or what David Easton calls, "creative speculation", in areas as intrinsically value laden as those concerned with human behaviour. That there has not developed a field of social engineering that is analogous to mechanical engineering and that social engineering does not stand in the same relationship to the social sciences as medicine stands to biochemistry is obvious and need not be laboured. The reason usually given is that prescription implies manipulation, and that social prescription implies the manipulation of human behaviour—a consequence considered anathema to liberal democratic values.

What this perspective overlooks, however, is that some degree of social manipulation is inescapable—a fact that was recognized by democratic theorists as different as John Stuart Mill and Rousseau. Attempts to shape individual behaviour already occur and are commonplace in the family, at school, in the workplace, on television, and in countless other forums, some benign and others less so. The failure to recognize social manipulation and to dismiss value-laden questions because they do not lend themselves easily to traditional modes of inquiry results in a tacit conservatism and acceptance of the status quo, a stance which is as inconsistent with liberal democratic values as is behavioural engineering.

This book, then, blends description, analysis, evaluation, and, occasionally, informed speculation in an examination of citizen participation in Canada. It attempts to bring the tools of the social scientist to bear on some of the important empirical questions that underlie the normative debate in contemporary democratic theory. Although much of the discussion that follows is fundamentally descriptive and based on a synthesis and reinterpretation of previous research, the questions posed and the arguments advanced extend substantially beyond the pale of previous studies and explore neglected aspects of an issue that is critical for understanding and evaluating the prospects for democratic citizenship in Canada. It will not be possible, of course, to address all of the myriad issues in this debate in a volume of these modest proportions. Rather, the purpose of this volume is to identify the central issues in the contemporary debate, summarize and interpret the available evidence, and provide an outline for future research—goals that are only slightly less immodest.

Inevitably, the progress of a book from conception to print depends on the efforts of a number of individuals in addition to the author. This volume is no different. I am especially indebted to the General Editor of the Canadian Controversies Series, Robert J. Jackson, for his support and guidance throughout. I am grateful as well to Alice Falcone, Harold Clarke, and Thomas Spragens for reading all or part of the manuscript and providing valuable criticism. David Campbell, Steven Haeberle, and William Ritchie laboured long, and for student wages, to assemble bibliography and data; Patsy McFarland, Susan Skillen, Joan Tregear, and Dorothy Weathers performed heroically, typing the manuscript from illegible copy; and Beverley Beetham and Virgil Duff edited the manuscript with patience and tact. I also am indebted to Richard Rose and the University of Strathclyde in Scotland for providing such a comfortable, and stimulating, environment in which to work and to the Duke University Faculty Research Council for financial assistance.

Finally, I owe very special, though quite different debts to Allan Kornberg whose work on Canadian political behaviour provides a benchwork for that which follows, and to my wife, Catherine, to whom this volume is dedicated.

WILLIAM MISHLER
1978

1. Participation and Democracy

The concept of democracy is a growth stock. Although once disparaged as an "agreeable form of anarchy" and a perversion of the proper form of government,[1] today it enjoys almost universal acclaim. It is embraced as fundamental by an extraordinary majority of the world's nation states (including many of the most authoritarian), and it serves as well as the organizing philosophy for most, if not all, of the various experiments in international and supranational government.

Canada, too, claims the appellation. The concept does not appear in Canada's fundamental document, the British North America Act, but according to R. MacGregor Dawson:

> The first and most important characteristic of Canadian government is that it is a democracy. . . . Government in Canada rests on the will of the people and is—ideally at least —at all times responsive to their opinions.[2]

Although an assessment of the extent to which the democratic ideal is practised in Canadian politics is a primary goal of this analysis, it is apparent at the outset, that whatever the truth in John Porter's contention that Canada "has a long way to go to become in any sense a thorough-going democracy",[3] the government of Canada stands among a relative handful of modern nations that can fairly claim to have embraced broad democratic principles. Regular elections, universal suffrage, representative political institutions, the toleration of opposition and at least certain forms of dissent, the existence of competitive political parties, and the protection of human rights are among the many obvious features which validate Canada's standing as a democratic polity.

It is not surprising, however, that the more popular the concept of democracy has become, the more its meaning has been debased. As T. S. Eliot observed in 1940, "When a term has become so universally sanctified as 'democracy' now is, I begin to wonder whether it means anything in meaning too many things. . . ."[4] Nor has the concept been clarified by its usage in the ensuing four decades. A philosophy capable of being embraced by political systems as disparate as those of the United Kingdom and Nazi Germany, the Soviet Union and the United States, the Republic of South Africa and Kenya, and Canada and Mexico is, literally, nonsense.

It is no easy task to restore meaning to a concept so long and so badly misused. Nor is this the place for such a monumental undertaking. The fabric of democratic theory is woven from many threads of which we will concentrate on only one (though perhaps the most important) in the discussion that follows. This is the thread of citizen participation.

Few aspects of the Canadian political system are as revealing of the nation's character and democratic spirit as the nature and extent of citizen participation in political life. For more than two centuries, democratic theorists have maintained that rational and informed participation is crucial to democracy and therapeutic to the state. It fixes the limits of government authority, mandates government action, regulates social conflict, and promotes political stability. Participation is said to be healthy for the citizen as well. It imparts a sense of personal power and self-control; it contributes to his self-esteem and sense of belonging; it increases his capacity for empathy and tolerance; very simply, it provides the citizen with the opportunity for moral development and personal fulfillment.

Ironically, the strongest challenge to the principle of participation has occurred very recently, at a time both when civic activism and democracy are very much in vogue and when many of the necessary preconditions for rational participation are finally being realized in Canada and in a small number of other nations. The most strident of these criticisms have been issued by contemporary democrats who admit the need for a minimum level of popular participation but emphasize that a heavy dose of non-participation and political apathy is healthy for democracy as well. These critics charge that too much citizen participation in politics jeopardizes stability and social order while threatening the substantive values of democracy. Besides, they contend, a certain amount of political apathy is inevitable and probably inherent in the nature of man.

The crux of the contemporary debate in democratic theory, then, centres around a complex and multi-faceted series of questions concerning the quality of public opinion and the structure, causes, and consequences of citizen participation and apathy. This volume attempts to answer these questions for Canada and in so doing to evaluate the function of political participation in Canada for both the citizen and society. To do so, however, requires a better understanding of the major themes and issues that occupy centre-stage in the democratic debate. The remainder of this chapter examines this controversy.

SOME BASIC ASSUMPTIONS

The roots of classical democratic theory are many, and emanate from a variety of rich but disparate soils. So diverse are its intellectual origins, according to Carole Pateman, "that the notion of a [single] 'classical theory of democracy' is a myth",[5] the perpetuation of which is responsible for much of the contemporary misinterpretation and distortion of important aspects of the classical theories. Although undoubtably correct, there are, nevertheless, sufficient common principles and ideas underlying the political theories of many of those commonly associated with the classical democratic tradition that some attempt at synthesis is warranted even if the resulting abstraction is somewhat idealized and oversimplified. In attempting this synthesis, it is useful to concentrate on the theory of John Stuart Mill, perhaps the best known and most influential of the classical democrats, adjusting and modifying Mill's formulation to take account of significant ideas propounded or elaborated by others.

In the utilitarian tradition of eighteenth-century liberalism, classical theories of democracy are, for the most part, procedural ethics concerned less with the substance of government decisions than with the process by which those decisions are made. Most of the classical theories are predicated upon an assumption that even if individual values are not relative, true only for the citizens who hold them, then at least absolute values cannot be known or communicated to others. Although they varied in their commitment to this first and most important principle, the classical democrats, Mill in particular, maintained that, lacking knowledge of universal truths upon which to establish political authority, individuals in society must be accorded maximum opportunity to pursue their own goals and self-defined values, and to do so in self-determined ways.[6]

Recognizing, however, that the pursuit of individual goals inevitably brings citizens into conflict, the classical democrats established the sum of individual values or majority rule as the basis for resolving disputes and maintaining public order. Conflicts were to be resolved on the basis of laws established by popular consent. Majority preferences were to be identified through citizen participation, and the widest possible involvement of citizens in the political process was to produce a synthesis of the diverse and relative values of individual citizens into a unified, if still not absolute, basis of authority.[7] Thus in classical theories of democracy, consensus replaces truth as the source of authority, and individual participation in the polity is the procedure that identifies consensus.

Besides providing the basis for resolving conflict, individual political participation was viewed by the classical democrats as a necessary condition for individual development and moral fulfillment. According to Rousseau participation was educational. It widened the individual's perspectives, enabling him to acquire the "moral freedom which alone makes man the master of himself".[8] Participation "forced man to be free".

For Mill, as well, the primary importance of participation lay in its benefit to the individual. Although Mill clearly believed that participation is a useful instrument of social regulation and decision-making, he argued in the conclusion of his essay, "On Liberty", that:

> The worth of a State, in the long run, is the worth of the individuals composing it; and a State which postpones the interests of *their* mental expansion and elevation . . .; a State which dwarfs its men in order that they may be more docile

instruments in its hands even for beneficial purposes—will find that with small men no great thing can really be accomplished. . . .[9]

Although Mill argued further that, "nothing less can be ultimately desirable than the admission of all to share in the sovereign power of the state",[10] he also recognized that the blessings of participation are not unmixed. If participation were to succeed in generating an effective base for political authority, Mill realized that citizens needed to possess certain virtues, principal among which were tolerance, rationality, and a spirit of civic activism. The classical democrats maintained that members of a democratic polity must have the capacity and motivation to become involved in a variety of political activities; they need to be capable of understanding a wide range of political questions; they must be intensely interested in political affairs; they must be well informed and behave rationally (as a minimum their attitudes and behaviour must be consistent); and they must be willing not only to tolerate the participation of others but to defer to the decision of the majority even when the will of the majority conflicts with their own.

Even the most optimistic democrats were not so naive as to believe that many citizens conformed to this model. What they did believe, however, was that most men had the *potential* to acquire these virtues but that the realization of man's potential depended upon proper education and the development of particular types of political and social institutions. Although Mill despaired of "the ignorance, the indifference, the intractableness, the perverse obstinacy of a people, and the corrupt combinations of selfish private interests armed with the powerful weapons afforded by free institutions . . ." he also believed that "among the foremost benefits of free government is that education of the intelligence and of the sentiments which is carried down to the very lowest ranks of the people when they are called to take a part in acts which directly affect the great interests of their country."[11] The classical democrats, in other words, did not believe that man is *by nature* a rational, political animal; but they were optimistic that rationality and a spirit of civic activism could be nurtured in man through an enlightened program of civic education. And they viewed the development of such a program as both instrumentally valuable for a just and orderly society and intrinsically valuable for the moral and intellectual development of the citizen.

THE MYTH OF HOMO CIVICUS

Several of the major assumptions of the classical theories came under attack almost as soon as they were articulated. Among the first to question the descriptive accuracy of the classical theories was Alexis de Tocqueville. Writing in the 1830s, de Tocqueville expressed the fear that if the substance of democracy were to be preserved, representative government had to be protected from what he perceived to be the authoritarian and anti-democratic passions of the masses. More recently, de Tocqueville's pessimistic impressions have been substantiated by more than two decades of survey research into the attitudes and behaviour of both elite and mass publics in Canada, the United States, and various Western European democracies. The overwhelming conclusion that emerges from these data is, as Robert Dahl expresses it, "Homo Civicus is not by nature a political animal."[12] Even in the most "advanced" industrialized societies, very few citizens appear to conform to the model of democratic man essential for the effective operation of a classical democracy.

Moreover, with respect to the democrats' requirements that political man be imbued with a developed sense of civic activism, research in Canada has confirmed what long had been suspected, that the interests of the average citizen range from crabgrass to hockey but rarely to politics. Indeed, one study concludes that fewer than five per cent of the Canadian electorate can be classified as full-time political activists, or political gladiators, in the sense that they are intensely interested in politics and regularly participate in the political arena.[13] At the other end of the continuum, however, up to twenty-five per cent of the electorate admit to such a high level of political disinterest or disaffection that they neither vote in elections nor pay attention to political matters. Nor are Canadians unusual for their level of political inactivity. The available evidence from the United States and a variety of other industrialized democracies indicates that other than voting, few citizens in any of the western democracies participate extensively in politics.[14]

Even in the act of voting the average citizen displays few of the virtues associated with the model democrat. For most citizens, voting has little rational basis. Voter choice, it is argued, is less a function of an informed, issue-orientation than it is of party loyalty, candidates' personalities, prejudice, or custom.[15] Indeed large segments of the public appear to lack even the most primitive or loosely structured belief systems of ideologies to guide rational decisions.[16]

In addition to demonstrating the discrepancies that exist between political practice and classical democratic theory, several critics of the classical model imply that the ideal of widespread citizen participation may not be ideal at all; that the classical theories are as flawed in their normative conclusions as they are in their empirical assumptions; and, as a consequence, that it would be both foolish and dangerous to promote higher levels of citizen participation in political life. On one level, it has been suggested that in many situations individual participation in politics is an unnecessary waste of the citizen's time: given the size and complexity of contemporary industrialized societies, the probability that one person's activities would influence specific political decisions is so slight that it does not justify the required investment of time and energy.[17]

In another sense, however, it is suggested that increased public participation is dangerous to society. According to this point of view, even if participation could be justified in terms of individual development, it would be undesirable for society because: individuals who currently do not participate are less sympathetic to democratic norms and thus more susceptible to authoritarian appeals than are current political elites; increased public participation probably would polarize existing social cleavages; and widespread mass participation threatens stability unless non-political institutions manifest similar participatory norms.

Although there is little data on these matters with respect to Canada, there is ample evidence from other nations to support the contention that mass publics tend to hold more authoritarian attitudes and are less tolerant of individual rights than are political elites. One study indicates, for example, that although most citizens in the United States agree with the fundamental values of democracy as abstract principles, substantially fewer of them are willing to endorse the application of these principles to specific situations. Moreover,

> Compared with the electorate, whose ordinary members are submerged in an ideological battle of poorly informed and discordant opinions, the members of the political minority [i.e., political elites] inhabit a world in which political ideas are vastly more salient, intellectual curiosity is more frequently demanded, attitudes are related to principles, actions are connected to beliefs, "correct" opinions are rewarded and "incorrect" opinions are punished. . . . The net effect of these influences is to heighten their [the elites'] sensitivity to political ideas and to unite them more firmly behind the values of the American tradition.[18]

Given the highly elitist nature ascribed to Canadian society, it is likely that differences in the fundamental political attitudes and beliefs of Canadian elites and masses are at least as wide as in the United States.[19] Indeed, they are probably wider. Assuming relatively weak public consensus on democratic norms, it is frequently argued that increasing public participation would mobilize individuals with little appreciation for the democratic "rules of the game", thereby exacerbating political tensions and jeopardizing political stability and social order. Far from serving the instrumental function of conflict resolution, political participation is viewed by its critics as destructive of social order and a threat to individual life and liberty. As Joseph Schumpeter expresses it, "the electoral mass is incapable of action other than a stampede." Therefore, both citizens and society need protection from mass actions.

Fortunately, according to the democratic revisionists, "where the rational man seems to abdicate, nevertheless, angels seem to tread".[20] Where the individual citizen is incapable of behaving rationally and in a democratic temper, competition and co-operation between political elites are sufficient to achieve essentially democratic ends. Relying upon the evidence previously

cited, the critics of widespread public participation advocate a
revised theory of democracy in which important political decisions are made by comparatively informed and tolerant elites
who are responsible to the public but who also are insulated to
some extent from the authoritarian impulses and caprice of
public opinion.

There are several variants of elitist theory. In one version,
called pluralism, it is generally argued that political decisions in
Canada are made by the leaders of various social, cultural, and
economic interest groups who compete with one another for
control in specific and fairly narrowly defined policy areas. The
elites are said to be drawn disproportionately from a narrow
range of society (principally the upper-middle class) and the
public's role in the process is confined largely to choosing between competing but highly similar elites in periodic elections.
Another version of elitist theory disputes the assumptions of
elite competition and pluralism. Proponents of the ruling-elite
version maintain to the contrary, not only that elites are
recruited from identical and unrepresentative backgrounds, but
that they exercise influence over a broad range of policy areas by
conspiring to eliminate competition and minimize the role of
public opinion. The most recent variant of elite theory, known
variously as elite accommodation or consociationalism, holds
that the leaders of Canada's various ethnic subcultures, obsessed
with the need to maintain political stability in the face of cultural
fragmentation, seek bargains at the elite level in an attempt to
compromise their different interests and thus to prevent these
differences from polarizing public opinion and producing conflict among the masses of the different subcultures.[21] Although
there is a considerable variety in elitist theory there also is
widespread agreement that: it is the elites who *do* govern;
political stability is best preserved by strictly limiting opportunities for citizen participation and by promoting a high degree
of public deference to political elite decisions; and maintaining
political stability is among the first and most important goals of
politics.

In the revisionist or "elitist" theories of democracy then, the
role of citizen participation is mixed. On the one hand, a certain
amount of participation—primarily in elections—may be valued

as a means of selecting elites and insuring at least a minimum level of accountability and responsiveness. At the same time, because of the belief that excessive participation can destroy stability, a certain amount of apathy also is desirable.

RESURRECTING THE INDIVIDUAL

Although few have challenged the validity of the revisionist's descriptions of how political decisions are made, an increasing number of questions have been raised with respect both to the normative implications of elitist theory and to the often explicit assumption that political apathy and an authoritarian personality are features intrinsic to human nature.

Underlying these criticisms is the belief that in attempting to reconcile the assumptions of classical democracy with the results of social science research, elitists have lost sight of the moral purpose of democracy.[22] The critics of elitist theory appropriately argue that the normative foundation of the classical model is its "sanctification" of the individual and its recognition that political participation is necessary for individual development. Even the democratic emphasis on the conflict-resolution function of citizen participation reflects the primacy of the individual. The amelioration of social conflict in democratic theory is not an *end* in itself but a *means* of creating an environment within which the individual will be free to pursue his own goals in his own way. According to one critic, however, "in the elitist version of this theory . . . emphasis has shifted to the needs and functions of the system as a whole; there is no longer a direct concern with human development."[23] The elitists have become conservative defenders of the status quo, committed to the preservation of political order as the highest, if not the only goal of government, and insensitive to the injustices which remain within society. Far from pursuing a value-free theory of democracy, it is argued, the revisionists have become the priests of a new and very different set of gods, and are willing to sacrifice political participation and individual moral development on the altar of government stability.

Leaving aside for the moment these normative issues, all of which will be examined in greater detail in subsequent chapters, the critics of the elitist model disagree as well with the assumption that apathy and intolerance are an inevitable part of human nature. The proponents of increased participation insist that apathy is not inevitable but results from the citizen's alienation from society and self and from the resulting sense of personal inefficacy and political powerlessness. These feelings of alienation are linked in turn to the individual's exclusion from effective participation in more basic social institutions. Denied opportunities to participate in basic social and economic institutions, it is claimed, the individual has not been provided sufficient opportunities to develop the attitudes and skills necessary for citizenship. Thus, rather than limiting participation because of the evidence regarding the authoritarian structure of institutions such as the family, the school, and the workplace, the critics of the elitist model reverse the argument and return to the theories of Mill and Rousseau to advocate the democratization of authority structures in basic social institutions as a means of stimulating greater participation in politics through citizenship education.[24]

In the critique of revisionism the anti-democratic values and authoritarian predispositions of certain segments of society also are attributed to limited opportunities for self-determination. Again, consistent with classical democratic theories individual participation is heralded by its contemporary advocates for its educational value. Participation teaches self-restraint and sensitizes citizens to the interdependence of individual and group interest. Involvement in lower-level social and industrial institutions instills an appreciation of democratic norms and invests the individual with the belief that he can control his own environment.

Although the evidence marshalled to refute the elitist theory by proponents of greater participation is sketchy at best and far from convincing, neither may it be ignored. Several studies have been reported, for example, which document the existence of a strong relationship between political efficacy and opportunities for participation in the family and the school. Others have demonstrated significant correlations between political efficacy and the citizen's commitment to democracy, and there is a small but growing body of evidence that worker participation in industrial management not only contributes to the individual's self-esteem but reduces feelings of alienation and even increases worker productivity.[25]

Beyond criticizing the elitists' conclusion that apathy is inevitable, several of the participatory democrats challenge even the observation that apathy is widespread. Although acknowledging that citizen participation in elections and campaigns is limited primarily to voting, the critics of the elitist model caution that most studies of participation and apathy define participation too narrowly, focusing only on participation in the electoral process. Leon Dion, however, cites nearly a dozen activities, in addition to voting, that provide opportunities for citizen participation, and his inventory neglects the vast array of activities which lie at or beyond the limits of socially sanctioned political behaviour.[26] Participation in protest marches or in political demonstrations, civil disobedience, refusing to pay taxes in protest of government policies, even the decision to "drop out" or abstain from participation in the political system can be construed as political activity. Yet none of these activities, even the clearly legitimate ones, are embraced by most working definitions of participation. Thus, the contemporary democrats contend that the question of whether man is apathetic or not remains unanswered.

Somewhat oversimplified, then, where elitist theory maintains that apathy and authoritarianism are natural and inevitable, the proponents of greater participation reply that man is basically rational but his intrinsically sociable and activist nature has been subverted by an authoritarian environment in which there are few effective opportunities for individual participation and self-determination in such basic institutions as the family, the school, and the workplace. Modern man, they argue, finds himself isolated and powerless; he has become alienated from nature, society, and himself. Consequently,

> progress for democracy lies in enhancing the actual freedom, initiative, and spontaneity of the individual, not only in certain private and spiritual matters, but above all in . . . his work. . . . All that matters is that the opportunities for genuine activity be restored to the individual. . . .[27]

TOWARDS A THEORY OF DEMOCRATIC POTENTIAL

Perceiving discrepancies between classical democratic theory and the "realities" of human behaviour, the elitists propose revisions in democratic theory to accommodate the imperfection of the citizen. In contrast, although acknowledging many of the same discrepancies, contemporary defenders of democracy insist that the distortions observed in citizen behaviour are not intrinsic to human nature but are products of the structure of authority in society. Their prescription is to preserve the classical theories of democracy and to restructure basic social institutions in order to increase the level and quality of citizen participation.

The question of man's nature is central to the contemporary debate and may be responsible for the current stalemate in democratic theory. However, rather than assume man's nature is immutable and debate its characteristics, it would seem to be more productive to focus on man's *potential* as a citizen. What man is able to become may be more important than what he is in resolving the central issues of this debate. In this regard, a return to the classical theories seems very much in order.

As we have noted, the optimism of the classical democrats did not include a naive belief that men were born to be, and forever remain, good citizens. Rather, their optimism stemmed from a faith in the potential of the citizen to develop the traits of democratic citizenship through proper education and experience. The elitists miss this point entirely. For their part, however, the modern proponents of greater participation have been content simply to decry the inadequacies of elitist theory while offering only vague and general alternatives.

What is needed is a synthesis of these two approaches; a mixture of democratic theory, empirical observation, and creative speculation—in short, an empirical theory of the citizen's potential for democratic participation. The contemporary controversy over the role of the citizen in democratic government cannot be resolved simply by discovering how much the citizen participates—although this question is important. Equally important are answers to questions concerning both the nature and causes of man's behaviour and his potential for change. Why doesn't the citizen participate more? What are the causes of political participation and apathy? Is the citizen capable of greater and more rational participation? How can participation be increased? And, if rational participation can be increased, what are the probable consequences of this participation for both the citizen and society?

In the pages that follow, this book attempts to piece together answers to these questions from the growing body of data and literature on citizen participation in Canada. Accordingly, chapters 2 and 3 are primarily descriptive and focus upon the related questions of who participates in Canada and in what activities. Chapter 2 defines the scope and dimensions of political participation in Canada and examines some of the historical patterns of citizen involvement. Chapter 3 explores the current level of citizen participation in a variety of political activities including voting and participating in political protests. In chapters 4 and 5 we continue this analysis by examining the psychological and social characteristics of both activists and non-participants. Chapter 6 takes up the question of citizenship training and education and includes a discussion of the dynamics of political socialization, while Chapter 7 evaluates the impact of participation upon the distribution of social resources as well as on the psychological development of the citizen. Finally, the concluding chapter returns to the broader issues of the democratic debate and assesses the prospects and probable consequences of directed social change.

NOTES
1. Plato, *The Republic*, trans. by F. M. Cornford (New York, 1968), Chapter xxxi, p. 285; and Aristotle, *The Politics*, ed. and trans. by E. Barker (New York, 1962), Book iv.
2. *Democratic Government in Canada* (Toronto, 1971), p. 3.
3. John Porter, *The Vertical Mosaic* (Toronto, 1965), p. 557.
4. *The Idea of a Christian Society* (New York, 1940), pp. 11-12.
5. *Participation and Democratic Theory* (London, 1970), p. 17, italics in original. The discussion that follows is heavily indebted to Pateman's excellent summary of the literature as it is to Dennis F. Thompson, *John Stuart Mill and Representative Government* (Princeton, 1976); Dennis F. Thompson, *The Democratic Citizen* (Princeton, 1970); and Dennis Kavanagh, "Political Behaviour and Political Participation", in Geraint Parry, *Participation in Politics* (Manchester, 1972), pp. 102-24.

6. John Stuart Mill, "Utilitarianism", in John Stuart Mill, *Utilitarianism, Liberty, and Representative Government* (New York, 1951), Chapter ɪ. All references to Mill are from this edition unless otherwise indicated.
7. Rousseau argued, however, that more than identifying consensus, participation served almost mystically to identify the general will. More than simply the will of the majority or even the will of all, the concept of the general will was elevated by Rousseau to the level of truth. In this, however, Rousseau departs rather significantly from the mainstream of classical democratic thought.
8. Jean-Jacques Rousseau, *The Social Contract*, trans. by Maurice Cranston (Harmondsworth, Middlesex, 1968), p. 65. Rousseau's theory of education is developed in *Emile* (London, 1911).
9. "On Liberty", p. 229.
10. "Considerations on Representative Government", p. 292.
11. Ibid., pp. 277 and 373.
12. Robert Dahl, *Who Governs?* (New Haven, 1961), p. 225. The literature on this addition to Dahl is vast. Among the classic statements of this position are Joseph A. Schumpeter, *Capitalism, Socialism and Democracy* (New York, 1947); and Seymour Martin Lipset, *Political Man* (New York, 1960).
13. Richard Van Loon, "Participation in Canada: The 1965 Election", *Canadian Journal of Political Science*, Vol. 3 (September 1970), pp. 376-90.
14. On the United States, see Sidney Verba and Norman Nie, *Participation in America* (New York, 1972). For comparative data, see also, Sidney Verba, Norman Nie, and Jae-On Kim, *The Modes of Democratic Participation: A Cross-National Comparison*, Sage Professional Papers in Comparative Politics, 01-013 (Beverly Hills, 1971); and Norman Nie, G. Bingham Powell, and Kenneth Prewitt, "Social Structure and Political Participation: Developmental Relationships", *American Political Science Review*, Vol. 2 (June 1969), pp. 361-78.
15. The classical statement of this position is Angus Campbell, *et al.*, *The American Voter* (New York, 1960). An excellent criticism of this argument from a Canadian perspective is Harold Clarke, *et al.*, *Political Choice in Canada* (Toronto, 1978), esp. chapters 8, 11, and 12.
16. Among the more important studies in this regard are, Philip E. Converse, "The Nature of Belief Systems in Mass Publics", in David E. Apter, ed., *Ideology and Discontent* (New York, 1964), pp. 206-61; and Herbert McClosky, "Consensus and Ideology in American Politics", *American Political Science* Review, Vol. 68 (June 1964), pp. 361-82. For comparable data on Canada, see Allan Kornberg, William Mishler, and Joel Smith, "Political Elite and Mass Perceptions of Party Locations in Issue Space: Some Tests of Two Positions", *British Journal of Political Science*, Vol. 5 (April 1975), pp. 161-85; and Lynn McDonald, "Attitude Organization

and Voting Behaviour in Canada'', *Canadian Review of Sociology and Anthropology*, Vol. 8 (August 1971), pp. 164-84.

17. See for example, Gabriel Almond and Sidney Verba, *The Civic Culture* (Princeton, 1963), especially pp. 473-90. Further support can be found in Anthony Downs, *An Economic Theory of Democracy* (New York, 1957); Mancur Olson, *The Logic of Collective Action* (Cambridge, Mass., 1965); and James M. Buchanan and Gordon Tullock, *The Calculus of Consent* (Ann Arbor, 1962).

18. McClosky, "Consensus and Ideology in American Politics", p. 375. Empirical support for McClosky's thesis is abundant. See, in addition, Dahl, *Who Governs?*, Chapter 28; Samuel A. Stouffer, *Communism, Conformity, and Civic Liberties* (New York, 1955); and James W. Prothro and C. M. Grigg, "Fundamental Principles of Democracy: Bases of Agreement and Disagreement", *Journal of Politics*, Vol. 22 (Spring 1960), pp. 276-94.

19. Porter, *passim.*

20. Bernard R. Berelson, *et al., Voting* (Chicago, 1954), p. 311.

21. The classic statements of pluralist theory are Robert Dahl, *A Preface to Democratic Theory* (Chicago, 1956) and *Who Governs?*; C. Wright Mills, *The Power Elite* (New York, 1956) remains the definitive treatment of the ruling-elite thesis; and Arend Lijphart, "Consociational Democracy", *World Politics*, Vol. 21 (January 1969), pp. 207-25, is the standard introduction to elite accommodation.

    Applications of elite theory to Canada are numerous. Among two of the best, John Porter combines the ruling-elite and pluralist position in describing the structure of elites in Canada while Robert Presthus, in *Elite Accommodation in Canadian Politics* (Toronto, 1973), adopts a consociational model.

22. There are a number of provocative criticisms of the normative basis of the elitist model. Among the best are Peter Bachrach, *The Theory of Democratic Elitism* (Boston, 1967); Pateman, chapters I and II; Christian Bay, "Politics and Pseudopolitics", *American Political Science Review*, Vol. 59 (March 1965), pp. 39-51; and Jack Walker, "A Critique of the Elitist Theory of Democracy", *American Political Science Review*, Vol. 60 (June 1968), pp. 285-95.

23. Walker, ibid., p. 288.

24. See, in particular, Bachrach, Chapter 7 and Pateman, chapters 2 and 6.

25. This literature is discussed at length in Chapter 6.

26. Leon Dion, "Participating in the Political Process", *Queen's Quarterly* (August 1968), pp. 432-47.

27. Eric Fromm, *Escape From Freedom* (New York, 1965), p. 299. For an excellent discussion of the concepts of freedom and alienation in democratic theory see Christian Bay, *The Structure of Freedom* (New York, 1968).

2.

The Growth of Democratic Citizenship in Canada

We took the position in the previous chapter that the contemporary controversy in democratic theory centres on a series of empirical questions concerning the nature and extent of citizen participation, the causes of political apathy, and the potential for change. Since existing patterns of political behaviour are legacies, at least in part, of laws and customs whose origins lie in the past, it is important to begin an assessment of the current structure of participation by reviewing the history of political participation in Canada and the growth of opportunities for democratic citizenship. Before this can be accomplished, however, political participation must be defined and its scope delimited.

WHAT IS POLITICAL PARTICIPATION?

Political participation is variously defined in the literature as: the manner in which the citizen relates to his government; taking part in the formulation, passage, and implementation of public policy; or those activities by private citizens intended to influence more or less directly the selection of public officials or the decisions they make.[1] Although the definitions agree that political participation entails some form of interaction between the citizen and his government, they differ not only in their scope, abstraction, and susceptibility to measurement, but, more importantly, in the types of activities they conceive as political. Whereas certain definitions conceptualize participation narrowly as the act of voting or taking part in various other aspects of electoral politics, others interpret the concept broadly, including "activities" such as saluting the flag, paying taxes, or simply maintaining a spectator's interest in politics and public affairs. Even the decision not to participate in politics is viewed by some as a political act since the decision determines the citizen's relationship with his government and influences, however indirectly, the selection of public officials.

Our conception of political participation falls somewhere between those extremes. Defined abstractly, the meaning of political participation seems unambiguous. Participation requires activity and politics defines the content or focus of action. Although conflicting conceptions of politics complicate the matter considerably, if we begin by accepting David Easton's definition of politics as the authoritative allocation of values for society, it follows that political participation is activity by which citizens take part in, or attempt to influence, the distribution of values in society.

Several aspects of this general definition are critical and warrant explanation. First, the stipulation that participation requires activity excludes those aspects of a citizen's relationship with government that are exclusively or primarily passive, symbolic, or psychological in nature. Many political attitudes, a sense of psychological involvement in politics in particular, undoubtedly condition behaviour and contribute to the nature and extent of political activity, but they are not part of that behaviour *per se* and thus are not encompassed by our definition. Relatedly, activities such as talking about politics, reading about politics, keeping current with political issues and public affairs, pledging allegiance to a flag or other political symbol, or feeling supportive of the government are largely symbolic in nature. They are usually not intended to influence the selection of government officials or decisions and therefore are not political activities.

Second, democratic participation must be voluntary. Activities such as paying taxes or obeying the law are excluded from our definitions since they are mandatory and citizens cannot reasonably be expected to abstain from them. Conversely, however, refusing to pay taxes or intentionally disobeying the law do fall within the definition *as long as they are intended to influence political decisions.* Indeed such activities are clear examples of participation since they require voluntary action with possible serious consequences for both the citizen and government.

Although participation is limited to voluntary activity, politics is broadly defined as the process of social decision-making. Political participation includes individual or group activity whether legitimate or not, direct or indirect, regardless of its actual effect as long as the action is intended to influence public policy or policy-makers. Obviously, a wide range of activities are encompassed by this definition. Voting, participating in political parties or politically oriented interest groups, campaigning for public office, writing letters to public officials expressing a point of view, signing a political petition, attending a political rally, marching in a political protest, participating in a general strike, even attempting to persuade someone else to do any of these things can constitute political action depending on the context in which the activity is undertaken.

ALTERNATIVE MODES OF PARTICIPATION

Given the diversity even in this abbreviated list it would be untenable to assume that political participation is all of a type, or that all forms of participation require the same resources, attract similar types of participants, or evoke identical responses. Yet this is the point of view implicit in most of the earliest studies of participation in Canada and elsewhere.

Following the lead of Lester Milbrath's pioneering work, Richard Van Loon contends it is possible to construct a hierarchy of political participation in Canada by arranging different types of activities along a single dimension representing the intensity of involvement demanded of the participant.[2] At the high-commitment end of the continuum are full-time, and frequently professional political activities which Milbrath and Van Loon call gladiator activities. According to Van Loon, these attract no more than five per cent of the Canadian public and include such time-consuming activities as running for or holding public or party office and soliciting campaign funds. Transitional activities are the next most demanding. A larger share of the population, perhaps as much as one-quarter, participate in these activities, occasionally working in political campaigns, attending political rallies, or participating in party activities. Approximately 75 per cent of voting-age Canadians take part in spectator activities—the least intensive category—consisting primarily of voting and discussing politics with friends (the latter activity is included in Van Loon's definition of participation but is excluded by the definition developed here). Many citizens, however (perhaps as many as 30 per cent), do not participate in any political activities and are usually—though sometimes incorrectly as will be seen—classified as political apathetics.

Although the unidimensional concept of participation prevailed for more than a decade, more recent research suggests that political participation, even narrowly defined, can be distinguished along several important dimensions. A recent study of electoral participation in Winnipeg and Vancouver, for example, reports that gladiator, transitional, and spectator activities are distinctive types which differ in kind as well as in intensity and require participants to possess different physical and psychological resources.[3] Using a slightly broader definition of participation (though one more limited than we have proposed) Sidney Verba and Norman Nie identify four modes of political activity in the United States, two of which—voting and campaign participation—are incorporated in Van Loon's conceptualization while two others are not.[4] Included among the latter are what Verba and Nie call communal activities and personalized contacts. These are defined respectively as: a) individual and collective behaviour of a generally non-conflictual nature directed toward achieving a social or collective good (i.e., writing letters to public officials or organizing a political action group to oppose public policy; and b) strictly individual activities directed toward achieving a personal good (i.e., writing a letter to a public official to expedite payment of personal unemployment benefits). Applying this framework to Canada in 1965 and again in 1972, Carole Uhlander confirms the multidimensional structure of political participation in Canada, although observing that the nature of the underlying dimensions changed slightly across the decade.[5]

In a similar analysis, excluding indicators of individual citizen contacts with public officials but adding several measures of participation in political protests, Susan Welch reports four distinct though related dimensions of political involvement.[6] Three of these mirror those in Verba and Nie's and Uhlander's analyses (voting, campaign, and communal activities). The fourth, however, was identified as a dimension of political protest and included such activities as taking part in legal protest meetings or rallies, refusing to obey "unfair" laws, and participating in non-legal demonstrations and protest rallies.

It would appear from the literature then, that there are, as a minimum, six inter-related types of political participation consistent with our definition: voting, campaign activity, holding political office, contacting public officials for individual goals, communal activity, and political protest. These are listed in Table 2:1, categorized both by the nature of the act (whether or not it is part of the electoral process) and by its intensity.

As it is employed in this discussion, intensity refers to several important aspects of a political activity including, in particular, the level of initiative the action requires of the citizen, the commitment of time, money, and emotional energy it demands, and the level of political conflict to which it exposes the individual. Voting, for example, requires only minimal initiative especially in provinces where voter enumeration is a government responsibility. Voting requires little time, no expenditure of money, and little emotional involvement, and, since voting takes place in private, the only conflict the individual is likely to experience is psychological in nature and largely self-generated. The act of standing for public office, on the other hand, requires extreme intensity. It demands an exceptional commitment of time, money, and emotional energy, generates a high level of frequently bitter conflict (often touching family and friends, as well as self), and assumes a high degree of personal initiative.

The significance of these distinctions is perhaps best understood if we recall some of the assumptions of the alternative models of democracy described in the previous chapter. In the purest form of democracy (typified by ancient Athens) the structure of citizen participation is assumed to be both wide and

Table 2:1   A CLASSIFICATION OF SIX TYPES
OF CITIZEN PARTICIPATION

		Electoral	Non Electoral
	High	Gladiator Activities	Political Protest
Intensity		Campaign Participation	Communal Participation
			Particularized Contacting
	Low	Voting	

deep. Citizens are required to participate extensively in all activities from the lowest-intensity, spectator, activities to the most demanding activities in the polis. If we plot the scope of this activity against its intensity, the pure form of the classical model assumes a structure similar to that diagrammed in Figure 2:1. In contrast to this model, however, both the elitist model of democracy and a model we shall call representative democracy (a variant of classical theory) assume that the scope of citizen participation varies inversely with intensity. In the elitist model, the structure of participation is broad at the bottom, tapering sharply to a narrow peak (Fig. 2:1). The number of citizens participating in the lowest-level activities is comparable to the classical model, but considerably fewer citizens participate in middle- or upper-level activities. Neither as open as the classical model nor as restricted as the elitist, representative democracy is broadly based and gently tapering. Although citizen involvement at the highest echelons remains the preserve of a small group of specialists, the elite stratum of the model is undergirded by a substantial group of citizens active in middle-range activities from working for political parties to lobbying political officials.

Given their differing demands on a citizen's wealth, energy, and initiative, alternative types of political activity can be employed by different citizens to register their political opinions. This possibility together with the tendency of previous research to focus primarily on electoral activity suggests that elitist models may have received unwarranted support. Indeed, a

Figure 2:1 ALTERNATIVE CONCEPTUALIZATION OF THE STRUCTURE OF CITIZEN
PARTICIPATION IN THE POLITICAL PROCESS

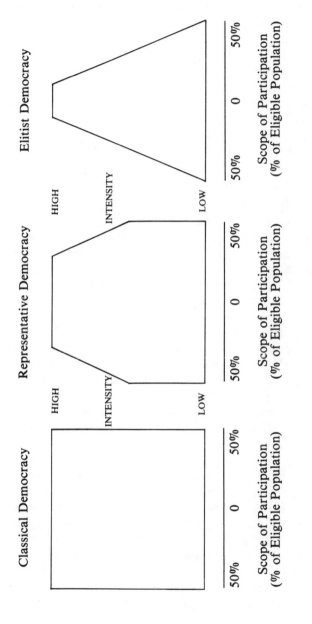

major criticism of the elitists is precisely that citizens, traditionally regarded as political apathetics, may actually be political
activists who choose to manifest their political concerns in non-
traditional or at least non-electoral forms.[7] Of course, once we
admit the possibility that citizens can fulfill their democratic
obligations in activities other than voting, we complicate the
task of assessing the structure of democratic participation. In
addition to measuring citizen participation in the electoral process, it becomes essential to consider the extent of their involvement in non-electoral political activities as well.

OPPORTUNITIES FOR PARTICIPATION

Broadly conceptualized, political participation is a product of
the interaction of individual opportunity and motivation. We
will consider the nature of this interaction, together with the
origins of motivation, in chapters 4 and 5. For now, however, it
is sufficient to recognize that citizens become active in politics
when, for whatever reason, they want to participate and possess
sufficient ability, legally and personally, to do so.

Although the opportunity for adults to participate in the
Canadian political process today is virtually universal, this has
not always been the case. Despite the nineteenth-century
liberals' faith in the rationality of man, opportunities for citizen
participation in many aspects of Canadian political life were
severely circumscribed at the time of Confederation and for
many years thereafter. The poor and propertyless, women, the
young, Indians, Inuit, and various religious sects among others
were systematically excluded from one or more categories of
political activity in the early years of the Dominion. Not only did
many of these barriers demonstrate remarkable resistance to
change but several persist today.

Restrictions on the opportunities for citizen participation are
of two general types: formal and informal. Formal impediments
are those established in law. These include restrictions based
upon sex, age, property, residence, citizenship, race, and
religion. Informal limits on participation are non-legal barriers,
although they may stem from the law, and usually are consequences of the inconvenience associated with a particular form

of activity. No one is expressly prohibited from voting by laws regulating the hours the polls are open, for example, but opportunities for some citizens can be effectively abridged if the voting hours coincide with the working day. The nature and severity of both formal and informal impediments to participation, and the historical development of opportunities for participation vary by activity.

VOTING: THE EXPANSION OF SUFFRAGE

Age, sex, and property requirements traditionally have been responsible for the greatest restrictions on voting in Canada. Of these, the requirement of property is most deeply rooted. Together with life and liberty, the right to acquire and protect personal property was viewed by many, liberals as well as conservatives, as fundamental, self-evident, and inalienable. Property owners were held to have a greater stake in the community, more stability, and less susceptibility to emotional and demagogic appeals than the propertyless masses. Further, it was assumed that wealth naturally accrued to men of talent. Individuals who were successful in accumulating property were believed to have demonstrated their superior intelligence, education, and talent and thus their qualification to manage community affairs.[8]

Given its foundation in democratic theory and, more importantly, the self-interest of the propertied class, the property requirement understandably was slow to fall. Prior to 1885 when the first Dominion franchise was enacted, six of the then seven provinces (all but British Columbia) maintained some type of property qualification. Over the next half-century, these requirements were gradually eroded, with Nova Scotia and Quebec finally abandoning them in 1920 and 1936 respectively. Prince Edward Island, however, held out against the egalitarian tide until 1963.[9]

Unlike property qualifications, restrictions based on sex derived less from democratic theory than from long-held prejudices about the physical, emotional, and intellectual inferiority of women[10] which date from as far back, perhaps, as the biblical account of Adam's rib and Eve's subsequent mischief in the Garden of Eden. Whatever the basis of sex discrimination, efforts toward the achievement of women's suffrage in Canada culminated in 1916 when Manitoba, Alberta, and Saskatchewan extended the franchise to women in provincial elections. Women's suffrage was established for Dominion elections in 1918 and for the remaining provinces, except Quebec, by 1925. Quebec, however, denied women the vote until 1940.

Opposition to voting restrictions based on age has never generated the sense of moral fervour characteristic of the fights against qualifications based on property and sex. Nor has it ever been seriously proposed to abolish age requirements altogether. The general principle, recognized by the classical democrats, restricted participation to citizens who achieved majority and whose rational faculties presumably had matured. Where disagreement has arisen, it has been with regard to definitions of when majority occurs. Owing largely to the contention of many that citizens who are old enough to fight for their country, pay taxes, and go to jail for disobeying laws are old enough to vote, mild pressure developed in the late 1960s and early 1970s to reduce the federal voting age from twenty-one to eighteen. The movement culminated in the passage of the Age of Majority Act in 1969. Today the legal voting age in Canada is eighteen for federal elections and for all the provinces save British Columbia where it is nineteen. A conservative estimate is that more than one million names have been added to the list of eligible federal voters since the 1969 change, increasing the size of the potential electorate by almost eight per cent.

Citizenship and residency requirements have not been as serious obstacles to participation in Canada as they have in other countries. Reflecting Canada's British heritage and continued membership in the Commonwealth, voting rights in federal and most provincial elections traditionally have been extended to British subjects and Irish nationals as well as to Canadian citizens. Although this practice of extending the franchise to British subjects in Dominion elections was terminated in 1975 by the Canada Elections Act, Canada retains one of the more liberal definitions of citizenship. Residency requirements in Canada also have been minimal. At the provincial level, the primary requirement is that citizens be residents of their provinces for at least one year (six months in Saskatchewan, British

Columbia, and New Brunswick) prior to the election and be residents in the constituencies on the day of the election writ.

Although once significant, formal restrictions based on race and religion also have been eradicated in Canada. The Inuit were granted the franchise in 1934 and Indians on reservations have been able to vote in federal elections since 1960. Citizens of Asian descent (the Chinese, in particular) experienced widespread voting discrimination especially in the western provinces as late as 1953; and although citizens who speak neither English nor French occasionally may encounter difficulties securing competent translators,[11] all of the most serious legal restrictions based on language also have been eliminated.

INFORMAL RESTRICTIONS ON THE FRANCHISE

As formal restrictions on voter participation have been eliminated, the importance of informal impediments has increased. Because informal restrictions result only indirectly from laws or formal regulations they are difficult to identify and measure. No one has been able to document, for example, the number of voters deterred by inclement weather. Nor do we know the number of Canadians who live in remote areas and have been effectively denied the right to vote because of the difficulties associated with getting to the polls. In the United States, where greater attention has been given to some of these concerns, research indicates that voting is affected not only by the weather and distance voters must travel to the polls but also by such mundane considerations as the complexity of the voting process and the length of the lines at the polls. None of these factors has the nature of a formal impediment to participation, but all of them increase the opportunity costs for voters and thus diminish the citizen's incentive to participate.

By far the most important informal impediment in Canada stems from the formal requirement that citizens be enumerated in order to vote. Although enumeration requirements in Canada are minimal compared to those in many other democratic nations, the United States in particular, it appears that between one and twenty-five per cent of the voting-age population, depending on the province, is denied the opportunity to vote because of enumeration procedures. Overall, in Dominion elections approximately five to ten per cent of the voting-age public cannot vote because of enumeration requirements.[12]

The effects of enumeration requirements on voting opportunities are illustrated most graphically through a comparison of the enumeration procedures and the resulting rates of voter enumeration in British Columbia *versus* the rest of Canada. At the federal level and in all of the provinces except British Columbia, enumeration is a government responsibility. Typically the government appoints enumerators who go door to door prior to each election collecting the names of the eligible voters in each household. The citizen's obligations in this system are minimal and are confined, largely, to responding to the enumerator's queries and initiating application for correction of the voters' list if, for whatever reason, the citizen's name is not included. In British Columbia, however, enumeration is the responsibility of the citizen who must take the initiative and visit the office of the Registrar of Voters in the appropriate electoral district. Although this procedure causes the potential elector in British Columbia only minor inconvenience (once registered, the name remains on the list indefinitely) it appears to discourage a surprisingly large number of potential voters. Whereas about 92 per cent of the voting-age public is enumerated in the other nine provinces, only 75 per cent appear on the voters' list in British Columbia. If the inconvenience is sufficient to deter close to fifteen per cent of the public from registering to vote, the potential impact of other, more imposing, informal restrictions is especially impressive.

PATTERNS OF VOTER TURNOUT

Despite the magnitude of the changes effected in the laws governing voting participation in Canada over the past hundred years, few of these changes appear to be reflected in aggregate patterns of voter turnout. Although the level of voter turnout in Canada traditionally has been high in comparison to the United States (owing largely to more restrictive voter registration requirements in the U.S.), it has been relatively low in comparison to several of the smaller European democracies.

The percentage of citizens included on the voters' list in Canada who have participated in federal elections since 1896 has fluctuated between about 60 and 80 per cent, reaching a peak in the elections of 1958, 1962, and 1963. Since the Second World War, turnout in Canada has averaged 75 per cent and has dropped below 74 per cent only three times since 1930—in 1940 when a blizzard on election day posed an unexpected impediment to participation in many areas, and again in both 1953 and 1974 when the elections were held in July and August while many citizens were on vacation (see Table 2:2).

Unlike the United States which has experienced a gradual erosion of voter participation since the late 1800s, Canada has enjoyed slightly increased levels of voter turnout since the Second World War. For purposes of illustration, Canadian history can be divided into three periods: 1896-1917—before universal suffrage; 1921-1945—the interwar period; and 1949-74—the recent postwar period. A comparison of average voter turnout across the three divisions indicates an increase from 71 per cent in the first two periods to 75 per cent in the third. Moreover, correcting for the sudden decline in the elections of 1921, 1925, and 1926 (resulting largely from the fact that women who were enfranchised in 1918 were slow to exercise their right to vote) reveals a gradual but steady growth in turnout at the federal level since 1896.

More illustrative, still, of the varieties of electoral behaviour in Canada are the patterns of voter turnout by province for both Dominion and provincial elections. Consistent with the aggregate, national trend, turnout in Dominion elections in most of the provinces, has increased across the three periods with only minor exceptions. In general, the greatest increases occurred after the Second World War, while the increases of the second period appeared to have been offset by the large numbers of newly enfranchised, non-voting women. Nevertheless, there are substantial differences in turnout among provinces for each election. As Scarrow points out,

The pattern of variation . . . since the election of 1930 appears to be directly related to the competitiveness of the electoral situation. . . . Prince Edward Island and Saskatchewan rank

Table 2:2 VOTER TURNOUT AT CANADIAN GENERAL ELECTIONS, 1896-1974
(Percentage)

Year	Ont.	Que.	N.S.	N.B.	Man.	B.C.	P.E.I.	Sask.	Alta.	Nfld.	Canada
1896	60	66	68	70	50	39	73				62
1900	85	69	75	76	65	59	**				77
1904	71	70	72	76	75	64	**				72
1908	69	68	73	77	80	58	**	**	**		70
1911	70	73	72	78	79	52	**	63	65		70
1917	75	76	80	89	79	80	80	74	76		77
1921	63	76	69	65	68	68	80	67	63		68
1925	65	72	70	61	68	75	75	57	57		66
1926	64	71	72	68	77	71	83	70	56		68
1930	69	76	83	78	72	73	89	81	66		76
1935	74	74	76	77	75	76	80	77	65		75
1940	69	66	71	69	75	78	78	77	64		70
1945	74	73	72	78	75	79	81	85	73		75
1949	75	74	75	79	72	69	85	79	69		74
1953	67	69	71	78	59	65	83	74	63		67
1957	74	72	81	81	74	74	85	81	73		74
1958	79	79	84	85	80	76	88	82	74	58	79
1962	80	78	84	83	77	78	90	85	74	57	79
1963	81	76	82	81	78	80	84	83	79	52	79
1965	77	71	82	80	74	75	88	80	74	79	75
1968	77	72	82	80	76	76	88	80	73	72	76
1972	80	76	80	77	75	74	86	79	76	69	77
1974	74	67	74	71	70	72	80	72	67	66	71

SOURCES: 1896-1965, John C. Courtney, ed., *Voting in Canada* (Scarborough, 1967), Appendix A: 1968-1974; *Reports of the Chief Electoral Officer, 1968-1974*.

as the most competitive provinces since 1930 and have recorded the highest average turnout; Quebec, Alberta, and Newfoundland have been least competitive and have recorded the lowest turnout.[13]

With respect to the levels of voter turnout in provincial elections, the pattern is nearly identical. Although data on provincial elections are more difficult to obtain, what evidence is available suggests a division of the provinces into two groups: those whose average turnout since 1949 has regularly exceeded 75 per cent, and those whose turnout has averaged less than 70 per cent. Of the high turnout provinces, Prince Edward Island, New Brunswick, Saskatchewan, Nova Scotia, and Quebec, all except Quebec also rank among the top five provinces in Dominion election turnout. Lower levels of provincial turnout have been the rule in British Columbia, Newfoundland (until 1971), Alberta, Ontario, and New Brunswick. Of these, only Ontario ranks in the top five provinces in Dominion turnout.

Unlike the United States where voter turnout falls off precipitously in state elections, turnout in provincial elections historically has paralleled that in Dominion elections. Since 1949, only Ontario, Alberta, and Manitoba have suffered substantially lower turnout in provincial elections. Nova Scotia, Prince Edward Island, and British Columbia have experienced slightly higher turnout in provincial elections. Again, these differences appear to be related to levels of party competition. This is illustrated most graphically in Newfoundland. Between 1949 and 1966 when Joseph Smallwood and the Liberal party dominated Newfoundland politics, electoral turnout averaged only 63 per cent. In 1971, however, following a series of political scandals involving the Smallwood regime, Newfoundland voters appear to have been mobilized by the possibility of a real electoral battle and voted in record numbers. Almost 90 per cent of those eligible voted in 1971 and nearly 85 per cent voted in 1972 when the Progressive Conservatives defeated the Liberals for the first time.

Historically, then, the structure of electoral participation in Canada has been broad and expanding at the base. Although inclement weather or the prospect of a landslide may discourage perhaps one-third of those who are on the voting lists and thus are eligible to vote, given good weather and a reasonable expectation of a competitive election, all but a tiny segment of the electorate—perhaps as small as ten per cent—have accepted the democratic responsibility of voting.

PATTERNS OF NON-ELECTORAL BEHAVIOUR

Impediments to citizen participation in the variety of political activities other than voting are similar in many respects to those that condition the opportunity to vote. Gladiator activities (i.e., running for office), in particular, are characterized by many similar restrictions. Depending upon the office, candidates may be required to meet formal qualifications based on age, citizenship, property, or residence. They may have to post a substantial deposit which is usually not refundable if the candidate falls short of a minimum percentage of the popular vote, and they may be disqualified if they are employed as government contractors or have previously been convicted of certain crimes or corrupt political practices.[14]

Informal limits on gladiator activities are even more numerous. Candidates for public office are expected (though not legally required) to reside in the constituency they represent and may lose votes if they do not. They must secure the nomination of one of the political parties if they are to have a realistic chance to be elected. They must have sufficient wealth or public visibility to carry them through the campaign. And even if these requirements are met, a candidate's electoral fortunes may still depend on a variety of factors beyond his control, including his age, sex, race, religion, and ethnic origin.

Transitional activities, such as campaign participation, communal activities, and contacting public officials, on the other hand, are restricted very little, if at all, by formal rules or regulations. Candidates for public office normally are grateful for the voluntary assistance of almost anyone regardless of age, sex, race, property, citizenship, residence, or almost any other qualification. There are few formal restrictions on participation in political interest groups and none at all on the frequency or content of citizen contacts with government officials. What restrictions do exist on these activities are largely informal and stem from the fact that certain individuals are better able, by virtue of their occupations, wealth, and personalities, to spend the time and money required to work in political campaigns or hold responsible positions in a political club or organization. Still others may feel constrained in communicating with public officials because of perceived limitations of language or literacy.

Political protest is probably the most restricted mode of political activity encompassed by our definition. Aside from the fact that violent forms of protest are illegal and, therefore, formally prohibited to all citizens, less extreme forms of protest, including the strictly legal ones, are limited by the demands they make upon the participants' time as well as by public opinion. Individuals who express their political beliefs through strikes, political demonstrations, sit-ins, and other forms of protest or civil disobedience jeopardize their jobs, risk expulsion from school or estrangement from family and friends, and frequently incur the moral indignation and disapproval of the public. Political protest, then, requires an intensity of commitment commensurate with that required of political gladiators and warrants classification as an elite form of political activity.

Unfortunately, little systematic evidence is available regarding the historical patterns of citizen involvement in activities other than voting. Given the greater obstacles to participation in higher-level activities, the evidence that can be gleaned from the limited volume of historical materials suggests that very few Canadians have ever participated extensively in any aspect of the political process other than voting. Opportunities for gladiator participation in particular have never been numerous and probably have declined with time. Given the relative stability in the small number of elected public offices in Canada combined with the continued growth in the population, even if every eligible citizen wanted to hold an elected office fewer than one per cent could have the opportunity.[15]

Similarly, although opportunities for participation in political parties, electoral campaigns, and political-interest groups have never been limited, there is little reason to believe that full advantage has been taken of them. On the contrary, with the exception of the CCF, and to a lesser extent, the NDP, participation in political parties and voluntary associations traditionally has been the preserve of a small cadre of political elites. Even membership in the organized labour movement has been relatively small. Although the first national labour union was organized as early as 1873, organized labour could claim a membership of only about 16,000 by the end of the 1880s, 150,000 by 1912, and 350,000 in 1939.[16] Total union membership is now just under two million, but the percentage of the working force holding membership in labour organizations has not exceeded 25-30 per cent until quite recently. Even if we assume that all members are active politically through their unions—an assumption that is clearly untenable—it cannot be said that this opportunity for citizen participation has even been fully used.

Reliable information on political protest in Canada is especially difficult to obtain. At best we can identify those periods in Canadian history where political discontent has approached crisis levels and attempt to estimate the extent of citizen involvement. Although the level of political violence historically has been relatively low in Canada, significant protests have occurred approximately every ten to twelve years.

It is estimated that between 40,000 and 200,000 French Canadians were members of organizations, such as Frères Chasseurs, and participated in the rebellions in Lower Canada in 1837 and 1838. Subsequently, in response to the enactment of the Lower Canada Rebellion Losses Bill, more than 1,500 English Canadians rioted in Montreal in 1849, burned Parliament, and virtually ruled the city for three days. In 1869, Louis Riel, self-appointed leader of about 10,000 Métis in the Red River area, seized Fort Gary and established a provisional government of Manitoba. In 1885, Riel led another group of 600-700 insurgents in Saskatchewan. They were quickly defeated by Dominion forces and Riel was subsequently executed.[17] Following on the heels of the discontent manifested during the Manitoba school controversy in 1916, more than 15,000 Canadians took part in the conscription riots of 1917; 30,000 workers left their jobs in support of the Winnipeg general strike in 1919; another 12,000-16,000 waged sympathy strikes in Vancouver in the same year; and, in 1935, a march on Ottawa which began in Vancouver to protest government inaction on unemployment culminated in a riot in Regina and the death of several protesters.[18]

More recently, Manzer reports that between 1948 and 1960, Canada experienced twenty-nine riots and more than one hundred armed attacks together resulting in the deaths of eight civilians.[19] His analysis of this period further indicates that much of the violence during this period can be attributed to the activities of several hundred members of the Sons of Freedom Sect of the Doukhobors in British Columbia. The 1960s witnessed still further political protest and violence instigated primarily by the Front de Liberation du Québec (FLQ) and later, the Army for the Liberation of Quebec (ALQ) and culminating with the reign of terror and the draconian War Measures Act of October 1970. Political protest during the 1970s has been somewhat less violent, but equally as pervasive. Strikes and demonstrations have been organized in protest of such diverse issues as the war in Vietnam, government anti-inflation policy, nuclear testing on Amchitka Island, and the visit to Canada of the Soviet premier, Aleksei Kosygin.

Nevertheless, despite the frequency of political protest in Canada it is reasonable to estimate that the number of Canadians participating in the most extreme forms of political protest has never exceeded ten per cent of the population and probably has averaged less than one per cent. The absence of historical data on citizen participation in non-violent protest activity makes it impossible to judge the extent of these activities in Canada with any confidence. However, we can speculate that they have been somewhat more extensive than the more violent and dramatic activities discussed above.

SUMMARY

Notwithstanding the contention of R. MacGregor Dawson that Canadian government is appropriately characterized as both representative and a democracy, the structure of citizen participation in Canada historically has conformed more closely to the elitist rather than the classical or representative models of democracy diagrammed in Figure 2:1. Political participation in

Canada traditionally has resembled a sharply tapered pyramid—broad and expanding at the base, much narrower through the middle range, more narrow still and shrinking at the peak. Moreover, although formal opportunities for citizen participation in many activities have expanded substantially since Confederation, the growth in citizen activity has not kept pace. Consequently, although three-quarters of the eligible Canadian public traditionally vote in federal and provincial elections, fewer than one-third of the public—and perhaps as few as ten to fifteen per cent—have ever participated in more demanding activities. Fewer than ten per cent—and probably closer to one per cent—have ever participated in the most demanding activities, such as running for public office or taking part in certain forms of political protest, whereas, upwards of fifteen to thirty per cent historically have been politically inactive.

Although the pattern of political activity in Canada compares favourably with those in other western democratic societies, the traditional structure of participation in Canada bears little similarity to the classical democratic ideal of widespread citizen involvement in all aspects of the political process or to the model of representative democracy in which full-time professional activities remain the province of elected representatives but in which citizens participate extensively in a variety of political activities of low and moderate intensity. Whether this pattern persists in contemporary Canadian society, and whether increased levels of participation in more intensive political activities are possible or, indeed, desirable given evidence of citizens' lack of tolerance, information, and rationality remain open to question and will be considered in the chapters that follow.

NOTES

1. Lester Milbrath, *Political Participation* (Chicago, 1965), pp. 1-4; Geraint Parry, "The Idea of Political Participation", in Geraint Parry, ed., *Participation in Politics* (Manchester, 1972), pp. 3-5; and Sidney Verba and Norman H. Nie, *Political Participation in America* (New York, 1972), pp. 2-3.
2. Richard Van Loon, "Political Participation in Canada", *Canadian Journal of Political Science,* Vol. 3 (September 1970), pp. 376-99. A recent edition of Milbrath's volume abandons the assumption of

unidimensionality. See Lester Milbrath and M. L. Goel, *Political-Participation,* revised ed. (Chicago, 1977), Chapter 1.

3. William Mishler, "Political Participation and the Process of Political Socialization in Canada". Ph.D. Thesis, Duke University, 1972.

4. Verba and Nie, pp. 56-81.

5. Carole Uhlander, "Political Participation of French Québécois: The Relationship of Political Cleavages to Activity", paper presented at the Annual Meeting of the Canadian Political Science Association, 1978, pp. 10-12.

6. Susan Welch, "Dimensions of Political Participation in a Canadian Sample", *Canadian Journal of Political Science,* Vol. 8 (December 1975), pp. 553-59.

7. See in particular, Leon Dion, "Participating in the Political Process", *Queen's Quarterly,* Vol. 75 (Autumn 1968), pp. 432-38.

8. The liberal argument in defense of property is expressed most clearly by John Locke in his *Second Treatise on Civil Government,* Chapter IV. However, liberal support for the role of property was not unmixed. Although John Stuart Mill acknowledged that, "property is a kind of test" of an individual's education, he nevertheless concluded that, "the criterion [of property] is so imperfect . . . that this foundation of electoral privilege is always, and will continue to be, extremely odious." "Considerations on Representative Government", p. 383. Early Canadian attitudes toward property—as was also the case in the United States and Britain—conformed more closely to the views of Locke rather than Mill.

9. T. F. Qualter, *The Election Process in Canada* (Toronto, 1970), pp. 5-6. The discussion that follows has been substantially informed by Qualter's excellent treatment of the subject in Chapter One. The definitive, though very dated, work on the subject is, Norman Ward, *The Canadian House of Commons: Representation,* second ed. (Toronto, 1963), chapters XII and XIII.

10. Indeed, Mill maintained that sex is "as essentially irrelevant to political rights as differences in height or in the colour of hair. All human beings have the same interest in good government . . . and they have an equal need for a voice in it to secure their share of benefits." "Considerations on Representative Government", p. 390. An excellent description of the history of women's suffrage in Canada is Catherine Cleverdon's, *The Women's Suffrage Movement in Canada* (Toronto, 1950).

11. Qualter, *The Election Process in Canada,* p. 12.

12. Dominion and provincial enumeration statistics through 1966 are from Qualter, ibid., p. 29, Table 1-5. A comparison of the total voting-age population according to the 1971 Census with the number included on the 1972 Voters' Lists reinforces Qualter's

observations and indicates that slightly fewer than 95 per cent of the voting-age population were included on the voters' lists.

13. Howard A. Scarrow, "Patterns of Voter Turnout in Canada", in John C. Courtney, ed., *Voting in Canada* (Scarborough, 1967), pp. 104-05.

14. See on the requirements for public office holders, Ward, *The Canadian House of Commons,* pp. 61-82, and Qualter, *The Election Process in Canada*, pp. 45-80.

15. Although opportunities for holding elected public office are somewhat greater at the provincial and local levels, in absolute terms the percentage of citizens with a mathematical opportunity to hold *any* public office in Canada is still quite small except in the prairie provinces (Saskatchewan, in particular). One study estimates that in Saskatchewan there are between 40,000 and 60,000 different elective rural posts that must be filled by the 125,000 farmers. There is, then, approximately one position available for every two or three farmers. S. M. Lipset, *Agrarian Socialism* (Berkeley, 1971), p. 245.

16. Figures from M. C. Urquhart and K. A. H. Buckley, eds., *Historical Statistics of Canada* (Toronto, 1965).

17. Figures cited in Mason Wade, *The French Canadians* (Toronto, 1955), pp. 190, 271, and 393-440.

18. Walter D. Young, *Democracy and Discontent* (Toronto, 1961), pp. 14-28 and 40-56.

19. Ronald Manzer, *Canada: A Socio-Political Report* (Toronto, 1974), pp. 74-84. See also Dennis Szabo, "Assassination and Political Violence in Canada" Supplement G in J. F. Kirkham, *et al., Assassination and Political Violence* (New York, 1970), pp. 700-14.

3.   The Participants

As we observed in Chapter 2, relaxation of legal restrictions has produced a steady, if leisurely, growth in the proportion of Canadian citizens who vote. Participation demanding greater commitment, however, has been relatively rare, although, historically, Canada has ranked among the most participatory political cultures in the Anglo-American tradition.[1]

But what about today? How does the current structure of political activity compare with the past? What is the nature of citizen involvement? How wide? How deep? And how do these patterns differ among the various regional political cultures that contribute to the richness and colour of Canadian political life? This chapter attempts to answer these questions and in doing so, to sketch a portrait of the current structure of citizen participation in Canada.

ELECTORAL PARTICIPATION: VOTING

Of the several varieties of political activity encompassed by our definition, electoral participation (including voting, campaigning, and running for political office) has been the most frequently studied. Voting, in particular, has preoccupied social scientists, in part because it is the most visible and most easily measured form of participation, but also because it is one of the few activities whose value is recognized by elitist as well as classical democrats. For many, voting is the symbolic essence of representative government and the *sine qua non* of responsible citizenship.

If voting were, indeed, the pre-eminent index of good citizenship then most Canadians would conform very closely to the democratic model. Although citizen participation in municipal elections is quite low the data on voter turnout in federal and provincial elections reported in Chapter 2 indicate, for example, that: almost 80 per cent of those included on the voter lists normally participate in Dominion elections; between 60 and 90 per cent vote in provincial elections, depending upon the legal and political situation in the province; and the level of voter turnout has increased since the turn of the century. In the most recent Dominion elections 76 per cent of those eligible voted in 1968, 77 per cent in 1972, and 72 per cent in 1974, a summer election.

Even more indicative of the extent of individual participation in successive elections (as opposed to aggregate turnout in a single election) is the evidence derived from interviews with a representative sample of eligible citizens immediately following the 1974 contest.[2] Eighty-five per cent of these respondents reported voting in the election. When asked to think back to the elections of 1968 and 1972, moreover, 90 per cent of those eligible at the time claimed they voted in 1972 and 89 per cent recalled participating in 1968. Over-all, 62 per cent of the respondents reported voting in all three elections; another 25 per cent said they voted in at least two; 11 per cent claimed to have voted in at least one election, while only one per cent could not recall voting in any election during this seven-year period. Although these figures undoubtedly have been inflated by faulty memories and the reluctance of some to acknowledge neglect of what many consider to be the citizen's fundamental civic responsibility, they are impressive none the less. Even allowing for response inflation, close to 90 per cent of those eligible to vote do so at least occasionally, or will not acknowledge that they do not vote.

Significantly, as well, the majority of those who did not vote in 1974 explained their absence from the polls in terms other than apathy or a general disinterest in politics. When asked, the largest percentage (forty per cent) said that they had been out of town or on vacation on election day; twelve per cent indicated they had simply forgotten about the election or were too busy to vote. Only seventeen per cent of the non-voters (three per cent of the entire sample) stated they were disinterested in politics or simply had not wanted to vote. Another thirteen per cent said they had been unable to make up their minds about the issues or candidates or felt their votes would not make a difference.

About two per cent claimed they had been overlooked by the enumerator and thus were not eligible and two per cent said they had refused to vote as a form of political protest. Excluding both those whose decision not to vote was a form of political protest (and thus constitutes a form of political activity) and those who would not participate for religious reasons or because they were out of town on election day, only about six per cent of the sample could be classified as true political apathetics. These results are typical of those obtained in similar studies. Based upon an analysis of voters and non-voters in a Vancouver riding during the 1963 federal elections, Laponce concluded that "Ten per cent is near the irreducible minimum for voluntary non-voters in the absence of serious legal or social sanctions for failure to vote."[3]

Although the evidence reported here is testimony to the quantity of voting participation in Canada, the quality of this participation remains suspect. As we outlined in Chapter 1, classical theories of democracy assume not only that citizens will participate extensively but that their participation will be rational and predicated upon substantial political information. The available evidence suggests, however, that many citizens are considerably more active in elections than they are rational or informed. A survey of public opinion three months before the 1965 election indicated that a quarter of the public were unable to name their sitting member of parliament. Fifteen per cent could not identify their MPs' parties, and only fifty-eight per cent had ever heard or read anything about their representatives. Even following the election, a substantial proportion of voters (twenty-six per cent) could not name the winning candidates in their ridings; fifteen per cent still could not identify their parties; and one per cent could not even recall the party for which they had voted—although the question was put to them less than six months after the election. Given their relatively low level of such basic information, it is probable that voters are even less informed about the candidates' ideologies and issue positions.

Still less evidence is available to support the assumption of voter rationality. Rationality, as was explained in Chapter 1, usually is defined in terms of the congruence between an individual's issue beliefs and political behaviour. The rational voter, it is argued, is one who studies the issues, develops a personal position on them, evaluates the candidates' positions on the issues, and votes for the candidate whose issue stands come closest to the voter's own. In fact, however, several studies have indicated that, although voters do tend to vote for the party or candidate closest to them on salient political issues, individual issue beliefs are highly inconsistent, and the relationship between issue beliefs and voting is weak.[4] When voters in 1974 were asked why they had voted as they did, only about half of those who said they were influenced by party leaders or candidates cited the leaders' or candidates' stands on the issues. The remainder reported being influenced primarily by the candidates' styles and personalities. Moreover, when asked to list personally salient issues, only 63 per cent responded by mentioning specific issues such as inflation, unemployment, etc.; 16 per cent listed general issues (i.e., disliked the party platform, liked the candidate's stand on the "economy", etc.); 17 per cent cited personality or leadership factors; and 3 per cent responded by noting vague generalities (i.e., it was time for a change, candidate "x" is for the little man, etc.). The reasons given by the small proportion of citizens who voted for a different party in 1974 than they had in 1972 confirm the comparatively low importance assigned to issues as opposed to personality and style in the voters' calculus. Only about one-quarter of the 14 per cent of those who switched parties cited issue-oriented considerations.[5]

In brief, although the extent of voting in Canadian federal (and provincial) elections approaches and occasionally exceeds 90 per cent of the eligible public, many of those who do vote display few of the attributes characteristic of the model democrat. For many citizens the act of voting appears to be regarded as little more than a civic obligation.

ELECTORAL PARTICIPATION:
CAMPAIGN AND TRANSITIONAL ACTIVITIES

After voting, participation in campaigns probably ranks as the most common form of political activity in Canada. Because election campaigns are relatively short, low-budget events in Canada (especially when compared to elections in the United States), candidates and political parties have a greater need to attract the voluntary participation of large numbers of citizens to perform the array of tasks, trivial and substantial, required for electoral success. As a consequence, opportunities for citizen participation in campaigns are extensive. Active membership in a political party, attending political rallies and meetings, contributing time or money to a campaign, even attempting to convince friends how to vote (though not simply talking with friends about politics) are parts of the process for which there are virtually unlimited opportunities. However, as the data in Table 3:1 suggest, opportunties for participation in these activities far outstrip the actual level of citizen involvement.

In general between 20 and 40 per cent of the public, depending on the election, report participating in political campaigns. About one citizen in twenty claims to be involved in a political club or as an active member of a political party. And fewer than one citizen in thirty reports giving money to a political party or candidate. Although the data also indicate that more citizens might be willing to contribute money or time if they were asked, only 26 per cent of respondents in 1965 and 35 per cent in 1974 reported being approached by a political party or candidate and only 5 per cent of the respondents in 1965 recalled being asked specifically to contribute money.

Although it is evident that most citizens never participate in political campaigns, it also appears that at least part of the reason is the relative absence of *perceived* opportunity. The problem is not an actual lack of opportunity. Citizens are not prohibited from participating. However, many citizens appear to be unaware of the opportunities available and are neither willing nor able to spend the time and energy necessary to find them. Although citizens' reports of what they *might* have done are, at best, imperfect indicators of what they actually would have done, it is at least reasonable to speculate that if candidates and parties were more effective in soliciting citizen participation, and if opportunities for campaign participation were more widely publicized, a somewhat larger proportion of the public could be mobilized for middle-range political activity.

Opportunities for participation in political parties and political clubs, like those available for participation in cam-

Table 3:1 REPORTED PARTICIPATION IN ELECTORAL POLITICAL ACTIVITIES IN THREE CANADIAN SAMPLES
(per cent)

	Canada 1965	Canada 1974*	Winnipeg/ Vancouver 1967
I. Participation in Election Campaign			
a. Attended Political Rally or Meeting	15	19	29
b. Tried to Influence Other's Vote	17	22	28
c. Put Political Sign on Car	**	16	18
d. Solicited Campaign Funds	01	**	02
e. Telephone Worker	**	**	07
f. Mailed Campaign Literature	**	**	06
g. Canvassed Community	**	**	06
h. Election Day Driver	**	**	06
i. Scrutineer (Poll Watcher)	**	**	10
j. Other	05	09	**
Participated in Any of Above	22	40	37
Would Work in Campaign if Asked	**	**	44
(N***)	(2610)	(1262)	(625)
II. Contributed Money to Political Party or Campaign	03	**	09
Would Have Given if Asked	23	**	42
(N)	(2610)		(625)
III. Member of a Political Club	04	**	04
(N)	(2610)		(625)
IV. Active Party Member	**	**	04
(N***)			(625)

*Percentage of respondents who said they "sometimes" or "often" participated in these activities.

**Question not asked of sample.

***Ns vary slightly within samples by question.

SOURCES: Data for 1965 and 1974 are based on national samples described in note 2. The 1967 data are based on interviews with a sample of voting-age citizens in the cities of Winnipeg and Vancouver. The latter were collected and made available by Allan Kornberg and Joel Smith in association with the York University Survey Research Centre (project 105).

paigns, are numerous and diverse. Yet, less than five per cent of the public take advantage of either. Even within such organizations, the level of participation varies widely. In a study of local party activists in Winnipeg and Vancouver, Kornberg *et al.* report that more than a third of those listed as holding the highest party offices claimed they spend little if any time on party affairs. Another 25 per cent said they worked for the party an average of only two or three hours each week, whereas 4 per cent of the respondents reported working more than twenty hours a week for thirty weeks or more during the year.[6] Similarly, a survey of student members of political clubs in Ontario universities showed 60 per cent of the members devoted fewer than three hours per week to club activities. At the other end of the continuum, 10 per cent of the members worked more than twenty hours each week and devoted more than half of their leisure time to club affairs.[7]

Part of the reason such a large percentage of party "activists" are so inactive in the organization may stem from the fact that participation in party activities does not insure an opportunity to influence the selection of party candidates or policies. Despite attempts by both major parties to develop more open and "participatory" convention machinery during the late 1960s, there is little evidence that the reforms adopted succeeded in expanding opportunities for *effective* participation by the party membership. To the contrary, Englemann and Schwartz maintain,

> The participatory wave in present day [Canadian] society is currently being accommodated by both major parties in . . . a rather carefully controlled fashion. Both parties have recently submitted to several conventions, questionnaires, to take the place of spontaneously presented resolutions. . . . The questionnaires are posed by the leadership; in the case of a governing party, this in fact means the Government. . . . Participation is effected, true expressions of opinion result, yet "the house" cannot lose. . . . Machiavelli could not have designed it better.[8]

With the possible exception of the NDP, political parties in Canada appear rather systematically to have subverted convention reforms in order to manipulate convention delegates and dominate the selection of candidates and the adoption of party policies.[9]

However, even when members have been accorded significant opportunities to participate in party affairs, the impetus for their involvement has included non-political as well as political concerns. Although few individuals become involved in party work because of motives completely divorced from politics, for a large minority of workers concerns about candidates and policies are outweighed by considerations such as the desire to improve business or social contacts, to experience the fun and excitement of the political game, to achieve recognition within the community, or to be close to people who are in the news and are doing important things.[10] Given the definition of political participation as activity *intended* to influence the selection of public officials or the decisions they make, it is arguable that those whose motivations for party work are primarily social or personal-economic do not meet this definition and are not political participants in a strict sense. Therefore, even the estimate that only five per cent of the public participate in party work is probably too high.

Samuel Eldersveld has observed that political parties are "minimal efficiency organizations".[11] His comment was directed at U.S. political parties but is equally applicable to political parties in Canada. The latter succeed very well in only one area—getting out the vote in federal and provincial elections. It could be argued, of course, that mobilizing voters is the parties' principal function and since they perform it efficiently they do not need to be concerned about involving citizens in political campaigns or in the party organization. Such a view, however, overlooks other party functions—including, in particular, the aggregation and articulation of citizen interests—whose effective performance requires widespread public involvement in such party-centred activities as the selection of candidates for public office and the establishment of party goals, policy positions, and platforms. Given the centrality of electoral activity in the structure of political participation and the classical democratic faith in the value of participation for self-development, the failure of parties to encourage greater citizen involvement in political campaigns and party life stands as a major defect of the Canadian party system, though one that is not unique to Canada.

ELECTORAL PARTICIPATION: THE POLITICAL GLADIATORS

Thus far in this discussion, we observed the generally high level of voter participation in Canada and argued that still greater participation is possible. We noted the modest level of campaign and party activity, but argued that greater participation is possible in this area as well. With regard to gladiator political activity, however, the evidence indicates not only that participation is limited but that the expansion of this activity is probably neither feasible nor desirable.

Gladiator activities are distinguished from other forms of electoral participation in that they tend to be full-time occupations requiring political professionals. Although it is reasonable to argue that the time required to hold an office in a political party or political club qualifies the occupants of these positions as political gladiators, as well, the classic form of gladiator activity in a democratic polity is running for public office. Not surprisingly participation in these activities is severely limited. Except in certain predominantly rural areas in Canada where as many as fifteen per cent of the adult, male community may hold public office (most of which are part-time positions),[12] the number of citizens who have actively sought either elected or appointed office probably has never exceeded five per cent of the adult population and probably has been closer to one per cent or less. Given both the continued decline in the ratio of offices to the number of voting-age citizens, and the practical requirement for candidates to be sponsored by one of the four largest parties, it is unreasonable to believe that the level of gladiator activity can be appreciably increased.

Nor is this necessarily a problem. Although we have maintained that universal citizen involvement in most political activities is desirable, elitist theories contend the effort required for gladiator participation could detract from the efficient performance of non-political functions in society and destroy the quality of political discourse. Rational discourse and problem-solving are difficult enough in small groups. They would be impossible if society operated as a committee of the whole.

NON-ELECTORAL PARTICIPATION: INDIVIDUAL AND COLLECTIVE

Opportunities for citizen participation in the political life of Canada are not restricted to those available through the electoral process. Although elections, political parties, and political campaigns accommodate the participation of large numbers of citizens, opportunities for both individual and collective action outside the electoral process also are numerous. As a minimum, citizens can express their opinions on political issues or seek assistance with politically related problems by writing to their representatives or other public officials. Collectively, as well, citizens can indirectly influence public policy by joining and becoming active in one of the numerous voluntary organizations and interest groups in Canada who augment their economic, social, professional, and community service functions with occasionally intense involvement in the political process. Indeed, individual participation in interest groups is, along with voting, the primary form of citizen involvement endorsed by many democratic elitists. According to this thesis, interest groups function to organize and articulate individual interests in the political process thereby providing important opportunities for indirect citizen participation. And because interest groups enable citizens to speak with a collective voice, citizen influence in government is held to be much stronger than would be the case if citizens were to address government individually and in an unorganized fashion.

Ironically, despite the fact that non-electoral activities tend to be freer of formal rules and regulations than most electoral forms of participation, fewer citizens participate in them. Although communicating with public officials is a relatively low-intensity activity, less than one-quarter of the public report ever having written to a member of parliament or other public official on any subject (see Table 3:2). Interviews with members of Canada's 28th Parliament (1968-72) indicate, moreover, that the content of these letters frequently is non-political. Although virtually all MPs receive a considerable volume of mail and other

Table 3:2   REPORTED PARTICIPATION IN NON-ELECTORAL
ACTIVITIES IN THREE CANADIAN SAMPLES
(per cent)

	Canada 1965	Canada 1974	Winnipeg/ Vancouver 1967
1) *Individual Activities*			
Ever Contacted Public Official/MP	**	16/24	**
Would Public Official Reply?	**	75	42
(N*)	—	(1262/2562)	(625)
2) *Collective Activities*			
Member of Voluntary Group			
Labour Union	24	30	**
Professional Group	17	**	**
Trade Association	4	**	**
Farm Organization	4	**	**
Other	21	**	**
Any of Above	55	**	`47
Ever Held Office in Voluntary Group	**	**	21
Work with Others to Solve Local Community Problem	**	26	**
(N*)	(2610)	(1262/2562)	(625)

*Although percentages are based on weighted samples, the actual unweighted NS are reported. NS vary slightly between questions.
**Question not asked of sample.

SOURCES: See note 2 and Table 3:1.

constituency correspondence each week, the majority (75 per cent) report that much of this correspondence involves requests for assistance with private and thus non-political matters such as securing unemployment insurance, veterans' payments, visas, passports, etc.[13]

Contrary to what appears to be the case for certain types of electoral non-participation, the failure of greater numbers of citizens to communicate with public officials does not appear to be the fault either of the political institutions involved or of public perceptions of these institutions. The public has very favourable impressions of the receptivity and responsiveness of public officials to constituent communications. When asked if they thought their MPs would read their letters if they wrote, three-quarters of the respondents in 1974 said yes. Of these more than 90 per cent felt the MPs would answer and try to do something about their requests.

Although a third of those citizens who had not written a public official were sceptical about the utility of such activity, public feelings of cynicism and inefficacy do not appear to explain the lack of citizen contact with public officials. Most MPs not only are willing to respond to constituent communications, but actively solicit such correspondence. Rather than waiting for constituents to write them, more than 90 per cent of the MPs in the 28th Parliament said they took the initiative, contacting constituents through mail questionnaires, newsletters, and radio and television talk shows in an attempt to understand constituent problems and opinions. Although it might be argued that MPs could do still more in this regard were their staff and office resources increased, it is doubtful, given the public's already positive assessment of public officials, that such parliamentary reforms would significantly increase the personal initiative or political involvement of constituents. In all likelihood, the public's lack of political initiative stems from more fundamental sources and must be sought in the personal experiences and social backgrounds of individual citizens.

We will have more to say about the determinants of participation and non-participation in subsequent chapters. Here our primary concern is to measure the extent of citizen participation across the range of activities included in our definition. In this regard, the evidence in Table 3:2 appears to demonstrate that the level of collective political activity is quite high. Canada is a nation of joiners. Between 50 and 60 per cent of the adult Canadian population belongs to at least one voluntary association (in Quebec, the figure is somewhat lower), and more than a quarter of the public belong to two groups or more. In terms of the percentage of citizens who belong to voluntary groups, Canada ranks ahead of such countries as Germany, Great Britain, Italy, and Mexico and on a par with the United States.[14]

On the surface it appears that the level of communal activity is second only to voting in terms of the number of citizens it involves in the political process. Such appearances are misleading, however, both because *membership* in an organization is not synonymous with *participation* and because not all participation in an organization is political either in consequence or intent. In the same way many citizens claim to be members of political parties but have never attended a party meeting or participated in any party activity, many citizens formally are members of voluntary organizations or interest groups but participate little if at all in organizational activities. One study indicates, in fact, that as few as half of the citizens who claim to be members of one or more voluntary organizations have ever been active in any organization to the extent of serving on a committee or holding an office.[15]

Nor is all activity within an organization political in content. Although politics is the *raison d'être* for many Canadian interest groups, for many others it is only a secondary or tertiary concern. Further, even in explicitly political groups, many, if not most members may be motivated to join by economic, social, or professional concerns rather than an interest in influencing the political process. Indeed, many members, even of highly politicized organizations, are unaware of the political activities of their group. In a survey of more than 600 directors of Canadian interest groups, Robert Presthus reports that fewer than ten per cent of the directors thought that the members of their group had joined the organization in order to influence government. And nearly three-quarters of the directors claimed that their average member knew little about the interest group's activities in the policy process.[16]

On the basis of this evidence, it appears that only a small number of citizens—probably fewer than 25 per cent—can be classified as political activists on the basis of the level and content of their participation in voluntary organizations and interest groups.

NON-ELECTORAL PARTICIPATION: POLITICAL PROTEST

Least studied of our categories of political participation is protest activity. Consequently, much of what is written about protest behaviour in Canada tends to be highly speculative, occasionally biased, and usually based upon analyses of protest "events" (aggregate behaviour) rather than upon the attitudes and behaviour of individual protesters.

Political protest activity can be distinguished along at least three dimensions—individual or collective, violent or passive, legal or illegal. As was noted in the previous chapter, because many forms of protest are illegal and many others, though legal, are condemned by public opinion, participation in political protests or demonstrations tends to be one of the more intense (i.e, "difficult to participate in") forms of political action. Nevertheless, as even a cursory review of the history of political protest in Canada (Chapter 2) makes clear, given sufficient cause, substantial numbers of Canadians have always been willing to take to the streets to demonstrate.

In recent years, much of the protest and political violence in Canada has arisen out of the continuing tension between the province of Quebec and Anglophone Canada. However, this certainly has not been the only cause. Protest also has occurred over matters as varied as the government's approval of nuclear tests on Amchitka Island, the treatment of Jews by the Soviet Union (occasioned by the visit of Alexei Kosygin to Canada in 1972), and the adoption of provincial medical-care insurance in Saskatchewan (the latter resulting in a doctor's strike that lasted twenty-three days), to cite only a few examples. Still, the level of political protest in Canada during the 1960s was substantially lower than in Great Britain and pales in comparison to the level of political turmoil in the United States (see Table 3:3). In the period from 1960 through 1967, Great Britain experienced more than three times as many protest demonstrations and riots, while the number of demonstrations and riots in the United States exceeded those in Canada by a factor of forty. And although Great Britain suffered only one death from political violence as compared to six in Canada, the United States experienced more than 260 such deaths during the same period. Even in per-capita terms, the number of political protests in the United States was almost four times that in Canada.

Accepting these figures at face value one might conclude that: the Canadian political culture is simply less violent than those of other Anglo-American nations; Canadians are happier with

Table 3:3 COMPARATIVE LEVELS OF POLITICAL PROTEST ACTIVITY IN CANADA, THE UNITED KINGDOM, AND THE UNITED STATES, 1960-67

	Canada	United Kingdom	United States
Number of Protest Demonstrations	23	88	118
Number of Riots	21	46	613
Deaths from Domestic Violence	6	1	266
Number of Times Government Sanctions Imposed	33	104	732
Ratio of Sanctions to Protests and Riots	0.75	0.78	0.42
Protests and Riots per 1965 Population (in 000,000)	2.24	2.45	8.89

SOURCE: Charles L. Taylor and Michael C. Hudson, *World Handbook of Political and Social Indicators*, 2nd ed. (New Haven, 1972). Tables 3:1, 3:2, 3:4, 3:5, and 5:1.

their government and have less cause for protest; or Canadian political institutions are more responsive to public needs and demands than those in the United States and Great Britain, thus obviating the need for participation outside of socially sanctioned institutions or processes. However, there are serious flaws in each of these explanations. The Canadian political culture may be less violent than the American with its frontier legacy, but it is not appreciably less violent than the British, and may be more so. Nor is there evidence supporting the contention that Canadian institutions are more responsive than others, or that Canadian citizens are more satisfied with their government's performance. On most indicators of performance the United States equals or surpasses Canada; the quality of life in Canada is high, about on a par with that in the United States; and Canadians are no more likely than Americans to manifest high levels of political support or confidence in their political institutions.[17]

Rather than indicating public satisfaction with the status quo, the relatively low level of political-protest activity in Canada may reflect greater restrictions on protest resulting from more stringent government regulations and more frequent resort to government sanctions against protest participants. Supporting this possibility is the observation that although the United States imposed a far greater number of sanctions against protest activities during the 1960s, Canada took action against a much higher *percentage* of such activities (75 per cent *versus* 42 per cent). This pattern is consistent with the argument of those who contend that Canada, historically, has demonstrated little tolerance for political protest, repressing dissent with whatever force was necessary whenever it occurred.[18] From the suppression of the rebellion in Lower Canada in 1838 to the proclamation of the War Measures Act in 1970, Canada traditionally has reacted swiftly and harshly against those who express their political dissatisfaction through protest demonstrations or political violence.

Notwithstanding the frequent use of sanctions in Canada, political protests remain a significant feature of the political landscape. In a survey of 560 white Anglo-Saxon households in Toronto, Susan Welch reports that six per cent of those interviewed claimed they had participated in "a political protest rally or march authorized by the government" some time during their lives; seven per cent claimed they had disobeyed a law they considered unjust; whereas two per cent said they had participated in protest rallies and marches which had not been authorized by the government. More than ten per cent of the sample acknowledged participating in at least one of these activities some time in their lives.[19]

Although impressive in their own right (note, for example, that the percentage of participants in these activities exceeds the percentage of those who claim to be party workers and campaign money contributors *combined*) these figures assume added significance in light of the range of protest activities *not* included in the survey. We have already observed, for example, that almost two per cent of the public say they have abstained from voting as a form of political protest. Many other citizens signal their discontent by signing petitions, voting for "extremist" or "hopeless" political parties or candidates, or by joining protest groups or organizations like the FLQ. Although reliable figures on the numbers of citizens who participate in these activities do not exist, we can speculate that the percentage of citizens who have taken part in some type of protest activity is probably considerably in excess of that reported here. It might be even higher, we suspect, if clearly legal and non-violent forms of political protest were less subject to government sanctions.

REGIONAL VARIETIES OF POLITICAL ACTIVITY

Although it may be overstating the case to argue, as do the authors of a recent article, that "Canadian politics is regional politics", there can be no denying their further observation that "regionalism is *one* of the preeminent facts of Canadian life".[20] The student who seeks to understand Canadian politics must begin by recognizing that different geographic regions in Canada were settled during different historical periods by people of radically divergent backgrounds. Although the provinces share the same federal government, they differ not only in their relations with this government but in the structure and operation of their own political institutions and processes. And the provinces continue to enjoy different levels of wealth, education, and industrial development as well. As a consequence, individual regions and provinces tend to view Canada's common history from very uncommon perspectives. Partly because of these differences, the provinces and regions of Canada have developed distinctive political cultures, which, it is argued, uniquely determine the political perspectives of their citizens and predispose the citizens to behave in distinctly regional ways.

In particular, Simeon and Elkins identify three general categories or types of political cultures based on the predominant set of political attitudes and beliefs in each province. At one extreme they list British Columbia, Ontario, Manitoba, and Anglophone Quebec as "citizen societies" whose members have comparatively high levels of both trust in Canada's political leaders and institutions and confidence in their ability to influence political decisions. On the other extreme are the "disaffected societies"—Newfoundland, New Brunswick, Nova Scotia, and probably Prince Edward Island—whose citizens' distrust of the government is equalled only by their generalized feeling of political impotence. French Canada, generally, and French Quebec, in particular, also are characterized by lower than average levels of political trust and efficacy combined with a tendency to be deferential toward authority while Saskatchewan and Alberta lie somewhere in the middle.[21]

Although these distinctions undoubtedly reflect broad differences and similarities in the political cultures and climates of the provinces, Simeon and Elkins are careful to note that several of these generalizations are relatively crude and all of them are oversimplified. Not only is the typology based on a series of questions administered more than a decade ago when the political situation in several provinces was substantially different than today, but most of the questions fail to distinguish citizen attitudes toward different levels of the federal system. It is reasonable to speculate, for example, that Francophone citizens in Quebec hold very different feelings of trust and efficacy about the provincial government of Quebec than the federal government in Ottawa. Anglophone citizens in Quebec also are likely to view government at the two levels quite differently (though in the opposite manner to that of their Francophone neighbours), and are likely to hold more disaffected attitudes toward both levels of government today in the wake of the 1977 victory by the Parti Québécois than they did in either 1965 or 1968 when the data on provincial political cultures were collected.[22]

Perhaps owing to the relatively crude nature of their typology, Simeon and Elkins report few significant differences in citizen political activity among provinces, almost none of which appear to be related to differences in political culture. Although certain types of campaign activity tend to be higher in the citizen cultures, other types are higher in the disaffected provinces. Extending their analysis to a wider range of political activities, the data reported in Table 3:4 reveal few consistent differences with regard to voting; suggest that citizens in disaffected societies are substantially more likely to participate in electoral campaigns; but indicate that on other measures of political activity, citizen participation tends to be higher in the citizen political cultures, especially British Columbia, than in the disaffected. These differences are generally small, however, and must be interpreted with caution.

Table 3:4 REGIONAL VARIATIONS IN CITIZEN PARTICIPATION, 1974
(per cent)

	Voter Turnout	Reported Voting	Campaign Activity	Political Club Membership	Contacted MP	Group Membership	Community Activity	(N*)
Nfld.	57	80	63	0	18	50	27	(102/51)
P.E.I.	80	93	50	4	22	38	18	(97/49)
N.S.	74	86	48	3	21	48	46	(180/87)
N.B.	71	88	47	1	17	36	33	(134/66)
Que.	67	82	41	5	18	52	19	(702/342)
Ont.	74	87	40	3	28	61	15	(702/343)
Man.	70	84	29	3	17	57	24	(113/59)
Sask.	72	88	37	13	29	53	44	(101/52)
Alta.	67	80	41	3	19	61	39	(179/85)
B.C.	72	86	35	7	33	61	19	(252/128)

*Data on Voting and Contacting MPs are based on entire sample of 2,562 respondents. Data on other activities are based on a half-sample of 1,262.

SOURCES: *Report of the Chief Electoral Officer, 1974* and the 1974 National Election Study (see note 2).

More striking than the variations in political activity between provinces of different political cultures are the differences apparent among provinces which presumably share the same culture. Over-all, there appears to be little relationship between political participation and political culture. Nor, for that matter, is there evidence of substantial relationships among the several types of political activity in that the position of a province on one indicator bears little relationship to its position on other measures.

Despite the variety of regional cultures in Canada, the effect of these differences on the patterns of citizen political activity appears to be minimal. Although citizens of different provinces and regions develop distinctive political attitudes and perspectives, it appears that political participation is influenced less by regional or provincial factors than by characteristics of the individual or sub-group. At least this is a plausible hypothesis that warrants further consideration in our analysis of the psychological and social determinants of participation in chapters 4 and 5.

The data on provincial variations in political activity are even more instructive of the limits of political involvement and the potential for expanding citizen participation beyond existing levels. By examining the extent of citizen involvement in similar activities in different provinces, it may be possible to gauge, however roughly, the upper limits beyond which we cannot realistically expect citizen participation to expand. For example, in our earlier discussion of voting and non-voting in Canada we concluded that increases in the level of electoral competition together with the elimination of the few remaining obstacles to voter participation might increase the rate of voting upwards to 90 or 95 per cent. Although the percentage of citizens nationwide who report voting in particular elections has, to our knowledge, never exceeded 85 to 90 per cent, the fact that 93 per cent of the respondents in one province, Prince Edward Island, report voting in 1974 (90 per cent of those on P.E.I.'s voters' lists actually voted in 1962) lends credence to our speculation. Lacking evidence to the effect that the electoral situation in Prince Edward Island is substantially different from that in the rest of Canada, we assume that there are no inherent obstacles to achieving equivalent levels of voting in the other provinces.[23]

Given the assumptions about citizen participation in the other types of political activities encompassed by our definition, the evidence in Table 3:4 warrants optimism regarding the potential for expanding the structure of political participation in Canada, especially in those large number of middle-range activities that lie between voting and full-time professional political work. If the experience of Newfoundland is a guide, it appears that nationally the level of campaign participation could be increased by as much as 25 per cent. The evidence from British Columbia, Alberta, and Ontario suggests that voluntary group partici-pation, communal activities, and communication with public officials could be increased by five to ten per cent each, while the experience of Saskatchewan suggests that participation in political clubs might be increased four-fold to just under fifteen per cent of the population.

SUMMARY AND CONCLUSION

The structure of political activity that emerges from this chapter resembles that which is diagrammed by the solid line in Figure 3:1—a structure broad at the base, narrowing sharply through the middle range, then tapering more gently toward the top. Aggregating the evidence regarding the extent of citizen partici-pation in both electoral and non-electoral activities, a reasonable estimate is that approximately 90 per cent of those who are eli-gible participate in the lowest-intensity activities in Canada, primarily by voting periodically in elections. Including those citizens who take part in political campaigns, communicate with public officials, or participate in the activities of voluntary organizations and interest groups, between 40 and 50 per cent of the public participate in middle-level or transitional political activities. Perhaps as many as ten or perhaps fifteen per cent participate in such high-intensity gladiator activities as running for public office, working for a political party or political club, or participating in some form of political protest activity.

Clearly, the structure of political activity in Canada bears

Figure 3:1 CURRENT AND POTENTIAL STRUCTURES OF CITIZEN PARTICIPATION IN CANADA

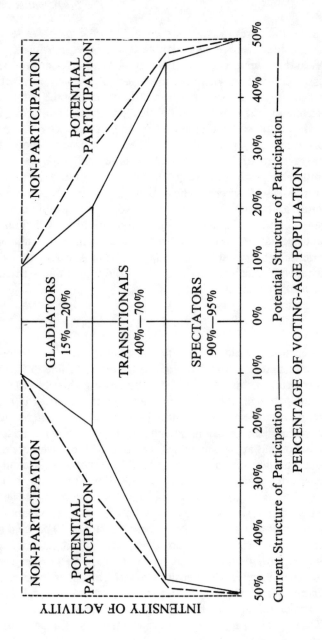

Current Structure of Participation ——— Potential Structure of Participation ------

faint resemblance to that presented in classical democratic theories. The Canadian citizen does not conform to the classical conception of *homo civicus*. However, it is equally apparent that the structure of participation in Canada deviates significantly from the elitist conception. If not a model democrat, neither is the average citizen the apathetic "political piltdown man" described in so much of the literature. Far from resembling spectators at a hockey game, but unwilling also to become gladiators in the political arena, a substantial number of citizens appear to be following a middle course, normally content to stand apart from the fray, observing the action, but willing also to commit themselves to at least limited political activity given sufficient opportunity and a reasonable expectation of success.

Not only does the level of political activity in Canada exceed the estimates of elitist theories but it appears as well that the potential for citizen involvement in Canada has not been fully achieved. Given higher and more consistent levels of electoral competition, still easier voter registration requirements, and more efficient political party organizations, the number of citizens who participate in moderate-intensity transitional political activities could be expanded by as much as 25 or 30 per cent, and both voting and gladiator participation probably could be increased by about five per cent as well. Of course, even were the full potential for citizen involvement to be achieved, the resulting structure of political activity would not resemble the classical model. The majority of citizens still would not participate in gladiator activities and a substantial number also would continue to abstain from transitional activities. The number of non-participants, however, would be reduced to about five or ten per cent, and up to two-thirds or, perhaps, three-quarters of the public would participate at least occasionally in one or more of the numerous activities in the middle range.

Rather than conforming to either the classical democratic model or the hierarchical model of elitist theory, the *potential* structure of political activity resembles more closely the model we have called representative democracy. In the latter, it will be recalled, maximum participation is prescribed in part-time amateur activities such as those included in the spectator and transitional categories, but gladiator activity remains the preserve of full-time, professional political specialists. Whether the expansion of citizen participation is feasible is a question that hinges on an understanding of the causes of participation. Whether it is desirable depends in part on whether the *quality* of participation can be increased apace with the quantity, and in part on the consequences of increased participation for both political stability and the psychological well-being of the individual. Subsequent chapters address these questions.

NOTES

1. Richard Van Loon, "Political Participation in Canada: The 1965 Election", *Canadian Journal of Political Science*, Vol. 3 (September 1970), pp. 396-99. For comparative data see Gabriel Almond and Sidney Verba, *The Civic Culture* (Princeton, 1963); and Giuseppe DiPalma, *Apathy and Participation* (New York, 1970).

2. Unless otherwise indicated, all data reported in this book pertaining to citizen attitudes and behaviour for the 1974 election are taken from *The 1974 Canadian National Election Study*. The data were originally collected and made available by Harold Clarke, Jane Jenson, Lawrence LeDuc, and Jon Pammett. Data on the 1965 election were made available by the Inter-University Consortium for Political Research and originally collected by Philip Converse, John Meisel, Maurice Pinard, Peter Regenstreif, and Mildred Schwartz. Neither the original investigators nor the Consortium bear any responsibility for the analyses or interpretations presented here.

3. J. A. Laponce, "Non-Voting and Non-Voters: A Typology", *Canadian Journal of Economics and Political Science*, Vol. 33 (February 1967), p. 81. In this earlier study, Laponce reports that 27 per cent of the citizens whose names appeared on the voters' lists failed to vote in the 1963 election. Of these, about one-quarter were what he terms forced non-voters (e.g., those who were ill, out of town, or ineligible to vote on election day). About two per cent of the nonvoting sample boycotted the election, nine per cent had been accustomed to voting when they were younger but now found the strain too great, and about sixty per cent of the non-voters (about sixteen per cent of the total sample) were classified as voluntary.

4. See, for example, Allan Kornberg, William Mishler, and Joel Smith, "Political Elite and Mass Perceptions of Party Locations in Issue Space: Some Tests of Two Positions", *British Journal of Political Science* (April 1975), pp. 161-85; and Lynn McDonald, "Attitude Organization and Voting Behaviour in Canada", *Canadian Review of Sociology and Anthropology*, Vol. 8 (August 1971), pp. 164-84.

5. For a somewhat different interpretation of these data, see Harold Clarke, *et al., Political Choice in Canada* (Toronto, 1978), chapters 8, 11, and 17.
6. Allan Kornberg, *et al.,* "Participation in Local Party Organizations in the United States and Canada", *American Journal of Political Science,* Vol. 17 (February 1973), pp. 23-47. A similar pattern was observed among the responses of the delegates to the 1973 Ontario Liberal Party Leadership Convention to a series of questions regarding the frequency of their participation in party activities. See Harold Clarke, *et al.,* "Motivational Patterns and Differential Participation in a Canadian Party: The Ontario Liberals", *American Journal of Political Science,* Vol. 22 (February 1978), pp. 139-41.
7. Harold D. Clarke, Allan Kornberg, and James Lee, "Ontario Student Party Activists: A Note on Differential Participation in a Voluntary Organization", *Canadian Review of Sociology and Anthropology,* Vol. 12 (May 1975), pp. 213-20.
8. F. C. Englemann and M. A. Schwartz, *Canadian Political Parties: Origin, Character, Impact* (Scarborough, 1975), pp. 223-24.
9. See, for example, the criticisms raised by J. Lele, G. C. Perlin, and H. G. Thorburn, "The National Party Convention", in H. G. Thorburn, ed., *Party Politics in Canada* (Scarborough, 1972), pp. 106-19; and J. McMenemy, John Redekop, and Conrad Winn, "Party Structures and Decision Making", in C. Winn and J. McMenemy, eds., *Political Parties in Canada* (Toronto, 1976), pp. 167-89.
10. On the motives for party work see Allan Kornberg, Joel Smith, and Harold Clarke, *Citizen Politicians: Political Socialization and Party Activism in Democratic Society* (Durham, 1979, forthcoming), Chapter 5.
11. *Political Parties: A Behavioral Analysis* (Chicago, 1964), p. 526.
12. S. M. Lipset, *Agrarian Socialism* (Berkeley, 1971), pp. 244-68.
13. Allan Kornberg and William Mishler, *Influence in Parliament: Canada* (Durham, 1976), Chapter 5.
14. Almond and Verba, *The Civic Culture,* p. 249; for comparable data on Canada see, Robert Presthus, *Elite Accommodation in Canadian Politics* (Toronto, 1973), pp. 20-63; and James Curtis, "Voluntary Association Joining: A Cross-National Comparative Note", *American Sociological Review.,* Vol. 36 (October 1971), pp. 872-80.
15. Data collected and made available by Allan Kornberg and Joel Smith in co-operation with the York University Survey Research Centre (Project 105). For a description of the study population see Kornberg, Smith, and Clarke, *Citizen Politicians,* Chapter 1.
16. Presthus, *Elite Accommodation,* pp. 286-87 and Robert Presthus, *Elites in the Policy Process* (London, 1974), pp. 92-95.
17. See, on these points, Ronald Manzur, *Canada: A Socio-Political*

Report (Toronto, 1974) and the data on public support for Canadian political institutions reported subsequently in Chapter 4.

18. See, for example, Judith Torrance, "The Response of Canadian Governments to Violence", *Canadian Journal of Political Science*, Vol. 10 (September 1977), pp. 473-96.

19. "Dimensions of Political Participation in a Canadian Sample", *Canadian Journal of Political Science*, Vol. 8 (December 1975), p. 554.

20. Richard Simeon and David J. Elkins, "Regional Political Cultures in Canada", *Canadian Journal of Political Science*, Vol. 7 (September 1974), p. 397. Emphasis added.

21. Using a different mode of analysis, John Wilson arrives at a very similar classification. Wilson distinguishes between what he calls the politically "developed" provinces (Alberta and Saskatchewan); those in a "transitional" stage (Quebec, Ontario, Manitoba, and British Columbia); and the "underdeveloped" provinces (Newfoundland, Prince Edward Island, New Brunswick, and Nova Scotia). "The Canadian Political Cultures", *Canadian Journal of Political Science*, Vol. 7 (September 1974), pp. 438-83. See also, Mildred A. Schwartz, *Politics and Territory* (Montreal, 1974), chapters 8 and 9; and Martin Robin, ed., *Canadian Provincial Politics* (Scarborough, 1972).

22. Evidence supporting this speculation is reported in chapters 4 and 6 and in Allan Kornberg, Harold Clarke, and Lawrence LeDuc, "Some Correlates of Regime Support in Canada", *British Journal of Political Science,* Vol. 8 (April 1978), pp. 199-216.

23. It is interesting to note in light of our earlier speculation regarding the possibility of increasing the level of citizen participation in Canada by improving the efficiency of political parties that Prince Edward Island, the province with the highest voter turnout in 1974, also is reputed to enjoy one of the most effective and efficient political-party systems in Canada. See Frank MacKinnon, "Prince Edward Island: Big Engine, Little Body", in Robin, ed., *Canadian Provincial Politics*, pp. 245-46.

4. The Psychology of Participation

Thus far in this discussion attention has centred on the nature and extent of political participation in Canada. It was argued in Chapter 1, however, that questions concerning the structure of citizen activity are only the first in a series of issues in the democratic debate. Central also to the controversy are questions about the causes of participation, the consequences of participation for the citizen and society, and the potential for change. This chapter begins consideration of causes.

EXPLAINING PARTICIPATION

As indicated in Chapter 2, political participation can be conceptualized, very broadly, as a product of two inter-related causes—motivation and opportunity. Citizens become active in politics when they want both to participate and to possess sufficient ability, legally and personally, to do so. Because motivation and opportunity are rarely absolute, participation depends on their relative strengths. Where the force of motivation exceeds the resistance posed by limitations on opportunity, citizens participate; otherwise, they do not.

We also distinguish in Chapter 2 between two general types of restrictions on opportunity—those formally established by law such as age or voter enumeration requirements and those which result from citizens' perceptions of the inconvenience of participating. As legal restrictions on opportunity have been eroded in this century, informal impediments to participation have assumed relatively greater significance. However, because informal restrictions tend to be psychologically based they are less susceptible to legislative reform. Consequently, although eliminating the few remaining legal impediments to opportunity might raise the level of political activity slightly, additional legislation is unlikely to expand the structure of participation appreciably. Motivation now appears the more important explanation of political participation in Canada.

Traditionally, motivational studies of political behaviour have adopted either a psychological or a sociological approach.[1] The former attempts to measure motivations directly and to explain citizen participation as a function of individual attitudes and beliefs. The latter also acknowledges the importance of motivations but tries to avoid what its proponents consider to be the "vagaries of psychological analysis".[2] It attempts to measure motivations indirectly by focusing on citizens' social and economic backgrounds and general life experiences. Underlying the second approach is an assumption that political attitudes are the footprints of experience and that citizens' personal histories catalogue those significant events that condition their current attitudes, thereby influencing both motivations and finally behaviour.

Far from being antagonistic the psychological and sociological approaches are complementary and are properly viewed as components of a single theoretical framework. Although focusing on different ends of the process, both implicitly assume a very simple model in which participation is conceptualized as a direct consequence of a set of individual attitudes whose origins are found in experience. This chapter examines the psychological bases of participation; the next will focus on sociological explanations.

PSYCHOLOGICAL INVOLVEMENT, POLITICAL INTEREST, AND INFORMATION

Given sufficient opportunity, political participation is a consequence of a complex set of individual attitudes about politics, society, participation, and self.[3] Although the variety of human action suggests that political decisions result from unique combinations of attitudes, there also are sufficient regularities in behaviour to support the belief that a common set of attitudes underlies similar types of political behaviour.

Among the most important of the traits distinguishing participants from non-participants in Canada is a cluster of political attitudes usually referred to as psychological political involvement. Simply defined, psychological involvement encompasses one's awareness of, interest in, and commitment to politics and public affairs. It is a broad-gauge determinant of political behaviour distinguishing participants from non-participants generally, and participants in activities requiring a high degree of initiative and intensity from those active in less-demanding forms. Indeed, so general are its effects that psychological involvement is frequently included—erroneously from our perspective—as part of the definition of participation.[4]

The level of psychological involvement in Canada has never been high. During the 1965 federal election campaign only about one-quarter of the electorate reported high levels of political interest. About forty per cent said they had at least a passing interest in politics, but nearly a third said they had little or no interest in politics at all. Moreover, the level of political interest has declined considerably in the ensuing decade. During the 1974 campaign only 30 per cent of the citizens said they were very interested in that year's election and fewer than 15 per cent reported high levels of interest in politics in general. In contrast, the proportion expressing little or no interest in politics increased from 30 per cent in 1965 to just over 40 per cent nine years later. Nor can this decline be attributed solely to the influx in 1974 of a large number of newly enfranchised citizens between eighteen and twenty years of age although political interest was substantially lower among young voters (55 per cent of whom expressed little or no interest in politics). Even excluding this youngest group, more than 40 per cent of the citizens twenty-one and over in 1974 reported minimal levels of political interest.

The relationship between political interest and participation is illustrated in Table 4:1. Among citizens who professed a high level of political interest in 1974, nearly 90 per cent reported voting in the general election. A nearly equal percentage of moderately interested citizens also voted, but substantially fewer of those reporting little or no interest went to the polls on election day. Nevertheless, that almost 80 per cent of this group voted as well suggests a moderate or high level of political interest may facilitate, but is not essential for, voting.

Table 4:1   THE EXTENT OF POLITICAL PARTICIPATION BY LEVEL OF
POLITICAL INTEREST
(per cent)

Activity	Low	Medium	High
Voting	80	88	89
Campaigning	27	46	65
Contacting MPs	15	27	38
Community Activity	13	21	39
(N* =)	(498)	(534)	(171)

*Voting percentages are based on a total sample of 2,445. All other activities are based on a half-sample of 1,203. NS are for half-sample and vary slightly between activities because of differences in missing data.

Since voting is among the least intense forms of political activity it has been suggested that the level of psychological political involvement might discriminate even better between participants and non-participants in more demanding activities. The evidence from 1974 confirms this expectation. Citizens reporting high levels of political interest were more than twice as likely as those with little or no interest to have written their MPs, three times more likely to have participated in community political activities or organizations, and nearly three times more likely to have worked in election campaigns. Indeed, nearly two-thirds of those in the highest political interest category worked in some capacity during the 1974 campaign (Table 4:1).

Because the *relationship* between political interest and participation has remained relatively stable during the past decade while the *level* of political interest has declined,[5] we might expect citizen participation to have declined proportionally, particularly since, as will be seen, the trend in political interest is symptomatic of a general decline in other motivations as well. That this has not occurred was evident in chapters 2 and 3. Far from declining, political participation in most activities has actually increased slightly during this period. The most plausible explanation for this is that political activity is habitual and self-sustaining. Although difficult to substantiate, it appears that once motivated to participate in some aspect of politics, citizens continue their involvement long after the original motivation disappears or is diminished. Participation becomes routine —something that the citizen does almost without thinking. If this speculation is correct, the consequences of declining interest may not be immediately apparent. Rather, declining political interest would be reflected in lower rates of participation only when current generations are no longer active and are replaced by citizens who have not developed the political habit.

The importance of psychological involvement as a motivation for political activity is reinforced by the fact that participation and psychological involvement tend to be reciprocal. Just as political interest spurs participation, political activity stimulates greater interest and wider activity. In a study of participants in the Action-Trudeau Campaign of 1968, Pammett reports that nearly twenty per cent of those interviewed said that their participation in the campaign enhanced their interest in politics. Nearly one-quarter also reported that their involvement had taught them a great deal about politics; nine per cent said they had become more aware of politics, although nearly fifteen per cent indicated that the campaign had caused them to become disillusioned with politics.[6] The latter reaction, however, appears to be atypical. Except for political protest, which is viewed by many as an alternative to other forms of political involvement, participation in one type of activity increases participation in the others.[7]

Closely related to the concept of psychological involvement, if not intrinsic to it, the level of political information also contributes to participation. Information increases motivation by heightening the individual's sensitivity to political messages in the environment, enabling him to understand a wider range of messages of greater subtlety and complexity. Information increases opportunity, as well. Citizens who understand the political process and how it operates are more likely to know where and how to take part in the political process. Finally, information enhances the quality of participation. It increases the likelihood that choices will be made rationally and is a fundamental prerequisite of democratic citizenship.

The extent of political information which Canadian citizens possess varies substantially. At a very simple level, most citizens possess at least a rudimentary understanding of the structure of Canadian government and the personalities that compose it. In a survey following the 1974 national election, for example, approximately three-quarters of those who were interviewed were able to identify the winning candidate in their constituency and 85 per cent were able to match the winning candidate with the winning political party. Considering the basic nature of this information, however, perhaps the more impressive observation is that 15 to 25 per cent of the respondents could not answer these questions.

Predictably, the level of political information declines as the sophistication of the question increases. Also in 1974, citizens were asked a series of questions testing their knowledge of the level(s) of government (federal, provincial, or both) with primary responsibility in such broad policy areas as education, foreign affairs, local government, hospital insurance, and unemployment insurance. Although almost 90 per cent correctly identified the federal government as having primary responsibility for foreign affairs and 80 per cent knew that the provinces are formally responsible for local government, nearly one-third of the respondents did not know which level is responsible for education policy and 40 per cent could not identify the level responsible for hospital and unemployment insurance. Over-all, about one-quarter of the respondents answered all five of the questions correctly, but nearly half "failed the test" in that they were able to answer correctly 60 per cent of the questions (three out of five) or fewer. Nevertheless, the level of information revealed in this survey was substantially higher than was found in a 1968 government information survey. In the latter a majority of respondents were able to identify the proper locus of jurisdiction in only three of fifteen policy areas.[8]

The extent to which citizens follow politics in the newspapers provides another indication of their interest in politics and serves as a primary explanation of the sophistication and extent of their political knowledge. Although newspapers are only one of several news sources in Canada—and not necessarily the most popular—it has been demonstrated that the electronic media (television, in particular) tend to have a stronger impact on the viewers' "emotional nerve ends" but newspapers are more effective sources of concrete political information.[9] In 1974, however, fewer than half of those interviewed said that they had closely followed the campaign in the newspapers. Another quarter read about the campaign at least occasionally but the rest read little or nothing. The percentage of citizens who attend to politics between elections is very similar. About 70 per cent read occasional stories about federal or provincial politics and slightly fewer attend to local news.

Interestingly, although newspaper consumption is a relatively crude indicator of political information, it distinguishes between participants and non-participants in most activities somewhat better than a more direct measure of basic political knowledge (Tables 4:2 and 4:3). Both correlate very well with variations in citizens' voting participation and the frequency of their communication with public officials, but there is little relationship between political knowledge and either campaign participation or community-service activities whereas the relationship between these political activities and newspaper consumption is striking: the most attentive citizens were twice as likely to participate in campaigns and to work to solve community problems than were the least attentive.

The reason for these differences may lie in the different types of political information elicited by the two types of questions. The political knowledge index reflects information about the basic structure of Canadian government, but newspaper articles are more likely to emphasize current political issues, events, and personalities. Although both types of information are necessary and desirable, current issues and events are more likely to seize the political interest of most citizens and thus to stimulate higher levels of political activity.

PARTISANSHIP, IDEOLOGY, AND CIVIC DUTY

Although many citizens participate because they are interested in politics, many others do so because of a need to express strongly held political beliefs or partisan loyalties, or to fulfill what they perceive to be the obligations of citizenship.

Table 4:2 THE EXTENT OF POLITICAL PARTICIPATION BY LEVEL OF
POLITICAL INFORMATION
(per cent)

Activity	Low	Medium	High
Voting	79	85	89
Campaigning	41	39	42
Contacting MPs	20	24	27
Community Activity	18	21	20
(N = *)	(279)	(649)	(275)

*Voting percentages are based on a total sample of 2,445. All other activities are based on a half-sample of 1,203. Ns are for the half-sample and very slightly between activities because of differences in missing data.

Few citizens possess sufficiently consistent political attitudes or constrained issue beliefs to qualify as ideologues,[10] but those who do seem to be strongly motivated to act in the political arena. Little Canadian evidence exists on the subject, but what there is suggests that ideology encourages both voting and campaign participation provided that at least one of the political parties—even a minor one—shares the citizen's preferences. However, those who can find no ideological accommodation through conventional forms of participation may turn to other means—primarily political protest. As one might expect, these participants are less likely to identify with one of the conventional political parties and more likely to be independents or supporters of more radical groups, such as the FLQ, or more moderate protest parties, such as the Parti Québécois, or, in its infancy, the CCF/NDP. We might also expect ideology to be a strong motive for gladiator participation. However, although political elites are more likely than the public to hold consistent political attitudes, they rarely *cite* such motives to explain their entry into political life or their subsequent activities in office.[11]

Of course, political beliefs do not have to be either radical or consistent to influence behaviour. A sense of loyalty to a

Table 4:3   THE EXTENT OF POLITICAL PARTICIPATION BY LEVEL OF
NEWSPAPER CONSUMPTION
(per cent)

Activity	Low	Medium	High
Voting	79	84	90
Campaigning	22	38	55
Contacting MPs	17	18	34
Community Action	12	19	27
(N* =)	(367)	(343)	(488)

*Ns vary slightly between activities because of differences in missing data.

political party is quite conventional, frequently non-ideological, and occasionally non-rational. Yet few aspects of a citizen's political personality contribute as much to behaviour.[12] Citizens with strong psychological commitments to political parties or their leaders are more likely not only to vote and participate in political campaigns but also to work for a party and become political gladiators. Even communicating with MPs and participating in community activities are related to the strength of partisan loyalties despite the fact that such activities are typically non-partisan (Table 4:4).

Although the relationship between partisanship and participation holds for all parties, those who identify with the two major parties are slightly more likely to vote in federal elections than NDP or Créditiste supporters. This may be because the latter are less sanguine about the prospects for victory and are unwilling to take the time to vote in what they perceive as a hopeless cause. NDP identifiers, however, are marginally more likely to participate in election campaigns, correspond with public officials, and become involved in community activities. Political independents, however, participate least of all. Contrary to conventional wisdom, their lack of partisan commitment appears to reflect political apathy or alienation (a concept discussed further below) more than a conscious decision to remain independent

Table 4:4 THE EXTENT OF POLITICAL PARTICIPATION BY
STRENGTH OF FEDERAL PARTY IDENTIFICATION
(per cent)

Activity	Low	Medium	High
Voting	82	84	91
Campaigning	31	40	53
Contacting MPs	21	20	29
Community Activity	14	21	25
(N = *)	(153)	(451)	(335)

*Voting percentages are based on a total sample of 2,445. All other activities are based on a half-sample of 1,203. Ns are for the half-sample and vary slightly between activities because of differences in missing data.

and to support particular candidates or parties depending upon their issue stands in each election.

In addition to those motivated by ideology and partisanship, many citizens participate out of loyalty to democratic forms or a belief that participation—voting in particular—is an obligation of citizenship. Although little attention has been given to these attitudes in Canada, the available evidence suggests that a substantial majority believe the right to vote should be exercised even if their choices have little chance for victory. Not surprisingly, then, a sense of civic duty is among the best predictors of voting participation in Canada. Interestingly, however, citizens who feel obligated to vote do not participate more frequently in other types of activities, perhaps because the concept of democratic citizenship propogated in Canadian textbooks and the media tends to equate voting with participation to the exclusion of other more intense forms of political activity.[13]

POLITICAL EFFICACY AND ALIENATION

Although citizens may be willing to vote when they suspect their efforts will be of little consequence, most are not willing to invest additional time and effort on more demanding activities without reasonable prospects for success. Consequently, political efficacy or the belief that one can influence political decisions through personal action, consistently ranks as a prime determinant of participation in Canada as it does elsewhere.

Political efficacy is a composite of two more fundamental attitudes: perception of opportunities for effective participation and a sense of personal political competence. Participation requires that opportunities exist, are recognized, and are believed to provide reasonable opportunities for success. Citizens who perceive effective opportunities must also believe themselves capable of exploiting them. If either component is missing citizens are unlikely to participate.

Significantly, the level of political efficacy in Canada is among the lowest in the Anglo-American democracies.[14] Although only ten per cent of those interviewed in 1974 agreed that "so many other people vote in federal elections it doesn't matter whether I vote or not", a majority did believe, "Government doesn't care what people like me think", and nearly two-thirds said, "those elected to Parliament soon lose touch with the people." Nor are citizens confident of their personal political capabilities. More than two-thirds of those interviewed in 1974 said, "Government and politics seem so complicated a person like me can't really understand what's going on," and a majority agreed that "people like me don't have any say about what the government does". In contrast, a 1974 election survey in the United States indicates that U.S. citizens were slightly more likely to find politics too complicated to understand and to believe that their congressmen lose touch with those who elect them, but they were slightly less likely to believe that public officials don't care about citizen problems and were substantially less likely to feel they were without a voice in politics.[15] Moreover, the survey in the United States was conducted at the end of a decade which had witnessed the assassination of three prominent public figures (including President Kennedy, his brother Robert, and Martin Luther King), a bitterly divisive war in Vietnam, the convulsions of the civil rights movement, and the resignation in disgrace of President Nixon barely three months before the survey—all of which reduced citizens' efficacy and trust to unprecedented low levels. Although the percentage of citizens in Canada who found government too complicated declined slightly between 1965 and 1974, those who felt government didn't care or who believed they had little say in government increased by a larger margin.

The consequences of such high levels of political inefficacy are evident in Table 4:5. Simply stated, Canadians with low levels of efficacy are less likely to participate in all forms of political activity than those few who feel reasonably confident of their personal influence. This is particularly the case with the more demanding activities. Citizens with high levels of efficacy are twice as likely as the least efficacious to write to public officials or participate in community affairs and almost half again as likely to become involved in election campaigns. Although efficacy also contributes to voting, the significant difference in this regard appears when the least efficacious are compared to all others. Even minimal levels of political efficacy appear sufficient to encourage citizens to vote, but substantially stronger feelings are necessary to promote participation in more intense activities.

Although attention thus far has centred on some of the overtly political attitudes influencing political behaviour, political attitudes do not exist in isolation. They are components of larger sets of attitudes and beliefs about government, society, and self, many of which—even the seemingly non-political ones—exert substantial influence on the nature and extent of citizen participation. It labours the obvious to note, for example, that most forms of political activity are group events which require extensive social contact. Although voting, writing to public officials, and atomistic forms of protest entail little contact, most other activities demand gregarious personalities. Citizens who dislike crowds or are uncomfortable in social situations are not likely to enjoy campaigning or running for office. Nor are they likely to be eager to become involved in community activities or to join a throng marching in protest of some government decision. Conversely, citizens who delight in such contact, enjoy meeting and talking to people, or find the dynamics of a crowd stimulating may be motivated to political activity by these sentiments alone. For these individuals, "politics may be just another club-type

Table 4:5 THE EXTENT OF POLITICAL PARTICIPATION
BY LEVEL OF POLITICAL EFFICACY
(per cent)

Activity	Low	2	3	High
Voting	73	86	88	87
Campaigning	30	37	43	48
Contacting MPs	16	19	25	34
Community Activity	12	20	22	24
(N = *)	(319)	(259)	(200)	(283)

*NS vary slightly between activities because of differences in missing data.

activity . . . the object of [which] may not be to influence the authoritative allocation of values for society but merely to provide satisfaction."[16] Although activity devoid of political intent is not "political" according to our definition, there is little doubt that a sociable personality is necessary for collective forms of political participation.

Even more important for participation than a sociable disposition are a sense of self-esteem and a strong identification with society. The absence of these traits is generally termed "alienation". The concept of alienation is shrouded in both controversy and confusion. The literature on the subject is prodigious and almost every study advances its own and usually idiosyncratic definition. In the narrowest sense of the term, alienation can be defined as estrangement—a feeling by an individual of being isolated from others, of not belonging to the political system, of being an "alien" in one's native society. In its broadest sense, alienation refers to a complex set of attitudes including feelings of powerlessness, meaninglessness, and normlessness in addition to social isolation and estrangement.[17] Strong arguments and some evidence have been produced in support of both positions each of which is useful in different situations. We shall use the broader definition of the term as a convenient surrogate for the host of more specific attitudes it encompasses. However, we shall not attempt to construct a composite index of alienation in Canada, not only because sufficient data are not available but also because the diversity of its components requires that the concept of alienation be disaggregated for analysis into more specific attitudes whose contributions to participation can be isolated and studied individually.

However the concept is defined, feelings of alienation in Canada are widespread. In addition to the high incidence of political inefficacy previously noted, Canadians demonstrate relatively high levels of political cynicism and normlessness compared to the citizens of other western industrial democracies. In 1965, for example, three-quarters of a sample of the Canadian electorate believed that "people in government pay too much attention to what the big interests want". A majority of these same people felt that "people running the government don't seem to know what they are doing" and more than a third had concluded that "government can be trusted to do what is right only some of the time". Moreover, nearly a quarter of those interviewed said, "people running the government are crooks" and one in three agreed that "government wastes a lot of the money we pay in taxes". By way of comparison, a similar battery of questions posed to a sample of citizens in the United States a year earlier indicated that fewer than half as many Americans thought that "government is pretty much run by a few big interests" (a slightly different version of the questions asked in Canada) or that government "doesn't seem to know what they are doing". A slightly larger percentage of Americans than Canadians felt that their government officials wasted a lot of tax money and that many of those involved in government were crooked. Yet, U.S. citizens were only half as likely as their neighbours to have reached the conclusion that government "can be trusted to do what is right only some of the time".[18]

Besides feeling powerless, cynical, and distrustful of government and politicians, many citizens expressed more fundamental dissatisfaction with life and pessimism about the future. About a third of a 1974 sample were at least moderately unhappy with the material aspects of their lives and only about a quarter of these felt the situation was likely to improve. Indeed, an equal number felt that the material quality of life was deteriorating, some claiming life is worse now than it was during the great depression of the 1930s. When questioned about life as a whole, 80 per cent expressed at least moderate satisfaction, although fewer than a quarter of these were willing to credit the government with contributing to the quality of life. It is worth noting as well that pessimism about life is increasing. Public satisfaction with life declined by ten per cent in the decade since 1965, a period during which the percentage of citizens expressing confidence in the future dropped by nearly half.

The political consequences of alienation are many and varied. According to one source,

> At the individual level . . . alienation [is] associated with a wide range of important political attitudes and behaviors, including revolutionary activities, innovative reformism, support for demagogues, rioting, non-voting, and protest voting, low or withdrawn political interest and participation, vicarious use of the mass media, participation in right wing activities, political party identification . . . [and] such "new politics" phenomena as campus sit-ins and national anti-war protest demonstrations as well.[19]

Although available data do not permit the development of a composite measure of alienation in Canada or an assessment of the impact of alienation on all forms of political activity, it is instructive to examine the impact of life satisfaction on voting. The concept of satisfaction is of particular interest given the conflict between the elitist contention that low levels of citizen participation reflect satisfaction with government, and the opposing point of view that inactivity reflects dissatisfaction combined with cynicism and despair. The evidence from 1974 clearly favours the second explanation. More than 85 per cent of the citizens who expressed general satisfaction with life voted in 1974 compared to only 77 per cent of those who were dissatisfied. Similarly, 88 per cent of those who were satisfied with the material aspects of their lives voted in this election compared to only 80 per cent of those who were not. Given the relationship previously observed between voting and other forms of political activity, we may assume (the data are not available) that less satisfied individuals also were less likely to participate in campaigns, write to MPs, or work on the community level. It may be true, as elitist theories suggest, that dissatisfaction with *particular* decisions or *specific* aspects of life (combined with general feelings of personal efficacy and trust) contribute to participation. But when dissatisfaction is generalized, as for many Canadians, inactivity is the political companion of alienation.

For most conventional forms of participation, then, alienation results in inactivity. This does not appear to be true, however, for some of the less conventional forms. In the case of political protest in particular, alienation may contribute to activity, especially among dissatisfied individuals with high political consciousness, a radical sense of efficacy (i.e., a belief in the efficacy of protest or violence though not of voting or other conventional activities), and an awareness of opportunities (made available by the presence of strong leadership) to express their discontent. The absence of systematic research on protest in Canada prevents detailed examination of this hypothesis, though the suggestion is consistent with research on right-wing protest in Quebec and on student protest activities in the United States and elsewhere.[20]

The final characteristic of the socially integrated or non-alienated citizen—a potential political participant—is a sense of identification with society. This typically takes the form of loyalties to important social groups, institutions, or symbols. Although Canada is a nation of "joiners", these loyalties tend to be parochial. Rather than identifying with national symbols or institutions, Canadians are characterized by strong regional and ethnic group loyalties. Indeed, a venerable thesis in the sociological literature holds the continuing mosaic of ethnic loyalties in Canada responsible for impeding the development of a strong national identity.[21]

Even though the parochial focus of citizen loyalties has little consequence for the over-all level of citizen participation, it does predispose Canadians to be disproportionately interested and active in local and provincial (as opposed to federal) politics. In addition to the relatively small decline in voter turnout from federal to provincial elections noted in Chapter 2 (and notwithstanding the rather substantial decline in voter turnout in

municipal elections), data (not shown) from 1974 generally indicate consistent levels of campaign activity at the local, provincial, and federal levels, and substantially higher levels of par-
ticularized contacting and campaign activity at the local level.

POLITICAL PERSONALITIES

Once a central focus of research the political consequences of
personality have claimed less attention in recent years.[22] Like the
concept of political culture which frequently serves as a "catch-
all" for differences between political systems which cannot be
explained by variations in more specific political structures and
processes, the concept of personality increasingly is regarded as
a rather vague and poorly defined aggregate of more specific
political attitudes and beliefs which are more profitably studied
individually.

Notwithstanding the validity of this perspective, the concept
of personality is useful because it underscores the inter-
relatedness of attitudes and provides a convenient summary of
the myriad psychological traits characteristic of various types of
political activists. It is this latter and very narrow function that is
of particular interest here. Accordingly, Table 4:6 profiles in
very general terms the political personalities of Canadian activists summarizing the political attitudes of participants in the
six types of activity encompassed by our definition.

Consistent with the traditional view that electoral activities are
unidimensional, the political personalities of voters, campaign
participants, and electoral gladiators display broad similarities.
Psychological involvement in politics, a feeling of partisanship
or commitment to ideology, a sense of political efficacy, and a
sense of social integration and rootedness in the community all
characterize, to varying degrees, participants in the electoral
process.

Substantial differences do exist, however. Voters in particular
are set apart in that their participation is private, involving little
commitment of time and energy. Voting places few demands on
a citizen's sociability, requires little sense of political efficacy,
and may even be discouraged by some ideologies. Campaign activities, in contrast, attract participants who are at once more

Table 4:6 PERSONALITY PROFILES OF POLITICAL PARTICIPANTS

Attribute	Electoral Participants			Non-Electoral Participants			Non-Participants	
	Voters	Campaigners	Gladiators	Communicators	Community Activists	Protestors	Apathetics	Disaffected
Psychological Involvement	Low/Moderate	Moderate	High	Moderate	Moderate	High	Low	Moderate/High
Partisanship	Low/Moderate	High	High	Low/Moderate	Low/Moderate	Low/Moderate	Low	Low
Ideology	Low	Low/Moderate	Moderate/High	Low	Varied	High	Low	Varied
Civic Duty	High	Low/Moderate	Moderate	Low	Moderate	Low/Moderate	Low	Low
Political Efficacy	Low	Moderate	High	High	High	High (but specialized)	Low	Low
Sociability	Low	Moderate	High	Low	High	Varied	Low	Varied
Alienation	Low/Moderate	Low	Low	Low	Low	High	Low	Moderate/High

politicized and more sociable. In addition, the campaign participant has a high level of personal political efficacy and may be motivated by a commitment to issues or ideology as well.

The personality of the electoral gladiator reflects many of these same traits, though typically in an exaggerated form. Citizens who run for public office or hold the highest offices in political parties often (though not invariably) develop an early, intense, and persistent interest in politics and public affairs. They are highly efficacious and gregarious, usually are more highly partisan and have more constrained sets of issue beliefs than either voters or campaign activists. And although citizen duty alone is unlikely to inspire gladiator activity, a sort of civic *noblesse oblige* does characterize many gladiators and undoubtedly contributes to their behaviour.

The personalities characteristic of non-electoral activists differ from those of electoral activists primarily in levels of partisanship, ideology, and sociability. Since partisan and ideological considerations provide few occasions for citizens to write to public officials or join community action groups, these attributes are, for the most part, irrelevant in this context. Community activities require high levels of social interaction and therefore a sociable personality; writing a letter to a public official does not. Both require, however, a sense of political efficacy, moderate to high levels of political involvement, and, particularly in the case of communal activities, civic-mindedness.

It is considerably more difficult to generalize about the characteristic personality traits of political protesters. Not only is less known about them, but what we do know suggests there are several types of protestors, each possessing a different set of psychological traits.[23] Political protest can be communal or individual. The latter, typically expressed in anomic acts of violence, is probably characterized by high levels of alienation, little sense of traditional efficacy, low sociability (in fact, by anti-social feelings), low partisanship, and perhaps, an unusual sense of civic duty or moral obligation. This type of activist may also have an intense, often radical, ideology and a strong psychological involvement in politics—or so we can speculate. Communal protesters have the same attributes in varying degrees except that theirs is a group activity requiring both a gregarious personality and a belief in the efficacy of group effort.

Finally, there also appear to be at least two distinct sets of personality traits characteristic of that segment of the Canadian public whose members do not participate in any type of political activity. On the one hand, a certain number of non-participants are properly classified as political apathetics. These individuals are characterized by few if any political attitudes, positive or negative. They evidence little or no interest in politics, few political beliefs (none sufficiently consistent to qualify as ideologies), and little sense of civic duty, political efficacy, or sociability. Although they do not identify with any political party, their independence is less a product of a conscious decision to remain non-partisan than it is a failure to make any choice at all. And although they do not identify closely with the political system, neither are they encumbered by feelings of political alienation and despair. Greatly oversimplified, they do not participate because they consider politics supremely unimportant—if they consider politics at all.

On the other hand, an equally large number of non-participants can be identified as disaffected. Although they, too, are characterized by low levels of partisanship and civic duty, they also may possess relatively strong and consistent political beliefs and highly sociable personalities. Such individuals are distinguished from other types of citizens, however, by moderate-to-strong political interest combined with low levels of political efficacy and moderate-to-strong feelings of political alienation. The politically disaffected care about politics but despair of any significant opportunity to influence the shape of political decisions through individual participation in the political process.

SUMMARY

Research on the psychology of participation in Canada is in its infancy. It is already clear however, that differences in political personality—in citizen attitudes and beliefs—can explain much of the variety in Canadian political behaviour. Nevertheless, although political attitudes are critical to understanding why some participate and others do not, their instrumental value is limited. Attitudes reveal little about the potential for increasing participation and less about how to achieve it. Thus our inquiry next will take us to a consideration of the origins of political attitudes and the experiences which produced them.

NOTES

1. Alternative conceptual frameworks can be found in Lester W. Milbrath, *Political Participation* (Chicago, 1965), pp. 29-38; M. Brewster Smith, "A Map for the Analysis of Personality and Politics", *Journal of Social Issues*, Vol. 24 (July 1968), pp. 15-28; and Robert E. Lane, *Political Life* (New York, 1959), pp. 5-7. Excellent reviews of the literature on voting determinants in Canada include Mildred A. Schwartz, "Canadian Voting Behavior", in Richard Rose, ed., *Electoral Behavior* (New York, 1974), pp. 543-617; and David J. Elkins and Donald E. Blake, "Voting Research in Canada: Problems and Prospects", *Canadian Journal of Political Science,* Vol. 8 (June 1975), pp. 313-25. Almost no research has been conducted on other forms of participation in Canada.

2. The emphasis on environmental explanations of behaviour stems in part from the view of behaviourists such as B. F. Skinner, that psychological constructs, such as attitudes, are non-empirical, can never be directly observed, and are thus not "scientific". B. F. Skinner, *Beyond Freedom and Dignity* (New York, 1971) and *Science and Human Behavior* (New York, 1953). For a critique of this perspective see Fred I. Greenstein, *Personality and Politics* (Chicago, 1965), Chapter 3.

3. The literature on political attitudes and public opinions draws relatively clear distinctions between such concepts as attitudes, beliefs, and opinions. Although useful and, at times, crucial these distinctions are largely irrelevant to this book. Consequently, although mindful of the differences, we will use the terms attitudes, opinions, and beliefs interchangeably throughout this chapter and the remainder of the volume. Readers interested in pursuing these definitional concerns should consult Robert E. Lane and David O. Sears, *Public Opinion* (Englewood Cliffs, N.J., 1964), or, for a more sophisticated treatment, Milton Rokeach, *Beliefs, Attitudes and Values* (San Francisco, 1968).

4. See, for example, Heinz Eulau and Peter Schneider, "Dimensions of Political Involvement", *Public Opinion Quarterly,* Vol. 22 (Spring 1956), pp. 128-42; Richard Van Loon, "Political Participation in Canada", *Canadian Journal of Political Science,* Vol. 3 (September 1970), pp. 376-99; and Mike Burke, Harold D. Clarke, and Lawrence LeDuc, "Federal and Provincial Political Participation in Canada", *Canadian Review of Sociology and Anthropology* (forthcoming).

86   POLITICAL PARTICIPATION IN CANADA

5. Van Loon, "Political Participation in Canada", Table VIII, p. 395.
6. Jon H. Pammett, "Adolescent Political Activity as a Learning Experience: The Action-Trudeau Campaign of 1968", in Jon H. Pammett and Michael S. Whittington, eds., *Foundations of Political Culture: Political Socialization in Canada* (Toronto, 1976), pp. 160-94.
7. Susan Welch, "Dimensions of Political Participation in a Canadian Sample", *Canadian Journal of Political Science*, Vol. 8 (December 1975), p. 556.
8. R. N. Morris, R. Morris, D. Hoffman, F. Schneider, and C. M. Lanphier, "Attitudes Toward Federal Government Information", Institute for Behavioural Research, York University (1969), p. 18.
9. The general argument is developed most fully by Marshall McLuhan, *Understanding Media* (New York, 1964). Support for McLuhan's thesis in Canada is reported by Stuart B. Proudfoot and Jon H. Pammett, "Children, Television and Politics: Is the Medium the Message?" in Pammett and Whittington, eds., *Foundations of Political Culture*, pp. 134-48.
10. See, for example, Philip Converse, "The Nature of Belief Systems in Mass Publics", in David Apter, ed., *Ideology and Discontent* (New York, 1965), Chapter 6. In Canada, in particular, see Allan Kornberg, William Mishler, and Joel Smith, "Political Elite and Mass Perception of Party Locations in Issue Space: Some Tests of Two Positions", *British Journal of Political Science,* Vol. 5 (April 1975), pp. 161-85, and Lynn McDonald, "Attitude Organization and Voting Behaviour in Canada", *The Canadian Review of Sociology and Anthropology*, Vol. 8 (August 1971), pp. 164-84.
11. Allan Kornberg, Joel Smith, and Harold Clarke, *Citizen Politicians: Political Socialization and Party Activism in Democratic Society* (Durham, 1979, forthcoming); and Allan Kornberg and William Mishler, *Influence in Parliament: Canada* (Durham, 1976), Chapter 2.
12. On the concept of party identification in Canada see, John Meisel, *Working Papers on Canadian Politics* (Montreal, 1973); Paul Sniderman, *et al.*, "Party Loyalty and Electoral Volatility", *Canadian Journal of Political Science,* Vol. 7 (June 1974), pp. 268-88; Jane Jenson, "Party Strategy and Party Identification: Some Patterns of Partisan Allegiance", *Canadian Journal of Political Science,* Vol. 9 (March 1976), pp. 27-48; and Jane Jenson, "Party Loyalty in Canada: The Question of Party Identification", *Canadian Journal of Political Science,* Vol. 8 (December 1975), pp. 545-53. The impact of party loyalties on voting is carefully assessed in Harold Clarke, *et al., Political Choice in Canada* (Toronto, 1978), chapters 5-8, 10, and 11.
13. William Mishler, "Political Participation and the Process of Political Socialization in Canada", Ph.D. Thesis, Duke University, 1972. See also, A. B. Hodgetts, *What Culture? What Heritage? A Study of Civic Education in Canada* (Toronto, 1968).

14. For a comparative treatment of the concept of political efficacy, see Gabriel Almond and Sidney Verba, *The Civic Culture* (Princeton, 1963), *passim*. Sources documenting the political importance of efficacy in Canada include Van Loon, "Political Participation in Canada", pp. 393-96 and Mishler, "Political Participation and the Process of Political Socialization in Canada", chapters 4-6. More recent research suggests, however, that the impact of political efficacy varies by province. See, Richard Simeon and David J. Elkins, "Regional Political Cultures in Canada", *Canadian Journal of Political Science,* Vol. 7 (September 1974), pp. 397-437 and Burke, Clarke, and LeDuc, "Federal and Provincial Participation in Canada", pp. 11-13.

15. Data from the *1974 American National Election Survey* were made available by the Inter-University Consortium for Political Research and were originally collected by the Center for Political Studies of the Institute for Social Research at the University of Michigan.

16. Van Loon, "Political Participation in Canada", pp. 393-94.

17. An excellent introduction to the many uses of the term is Richard Schacht's *Alienation* (New York, 1970). A strong case for a narrow definition is made by David C. Schwartz, *Political Alienation and Political Behavior* (Chicago, 1973), Chapter 1. The broader definition of alienation is that of Melvin Seeman, "On the Meaning of Alienation", *American Sociological Review,* Vol. 24 (December 1959), pp. 783-89.

18. Canadian and U.S. figures cited in Mildred Schwartz, *Politics and Territory* (Montreal, 1974), p. 208, Table 8:5. Comparable Canadian data for 1974 are not available.

19. Schwartz, ibid., p. 3.

20. In defense of these propositions, see Michael B. Stein, *The Dynamics of Right-Wing Protest: A Political Analysis of Social Credit in Quebec* (Toronto, 1973), esp. chapters 1, 6, and 7. See also Simeon and Elkins, "Regional Political Cultures in Canada", p. 436 and, for a comparative perspective, Giuseppe DiPalma, *Apathy and Participation* (New York, 1970), p. 116.

21. For the classic statement of this thesis see John Porter, *The Vertical Mosaic* (Toronto, 1965). See also Mildred Schwartz, *Public Opinion and Canadian Identity* (Berkeley, 1967); and George Grant, *Lament for a Nation* (Toronto, 1970).

22. The literature on personality and politics is voluminous. For an introduction to the area see Fred Greenstein, *Personality and Politics*.

23. Stein, *The Dynamics of Right-Wing Protest,* chapters 6 and 7. For an excellent summary of the literature on the origins of political protest and other unconventional forms of political activity, though from a predominantly U.S. perspective, see H. T. Reynolds, *Politics and the Common Man* (Homewood, Ill., 1974), chapters 7 and 8.

5. The Sociology of Participation

The motivation to participate in politics, we have suggested, is an extension of political personality. Citizens are not born with fully developed political attitudes; nor are they predisposed from birth to be voters, political gladiators, protesters, or non-participants. Our view, expressed in Chapter 4, is that attitudes and behaviour are learned. Personality is the sum and consequence of the frequently random circumstances and events which citizens experience, imperfectly perceive, and recall throughout life. We will have more to say about the process of political learning in a subsequent chapter. This chapter examines some of the experiences which provide the substance of the process and further explain why some citizens participate and others do not.

OCCUPATION, CLASS, AND SOCIAL STATUS

Among the many life experiences which nurture political personality, few have the potential to be as important as those associated with an individual's occupation and consequent position in society. Social and economic circumstances influence behaviour in two ways: they structure political opportunity and they shape the development of political attitudes thereby influencing motivations. Specifically, occupation and social status substantially determine the resources available for political activity. They influence perceptions of the personal importance of politics, the susceptibility of political decisions to individual effort and influence and, thus, the rationality of individual political effort. Citizens with higher status occupations are more likely to be viewed as opinion leaders in the community, to feel they have a stake in the political system, and to know and be known by public officials and political decision-makers. The

theory, simply stated, is that citizens with the highest status occupations are exposed to more political stimuli, have greater
political skills, and experience a wider range of political opportunities.[1]

Notwithstanding the appeal of this perspective or the manifest
importance of social class in other nations, it frequently is
argued that Canada is an exception. According to a popular
thesis, the political significance of class in Canada is diminished
by the over-riding importance of region and ethnicity.[2] Because
they are preoccupied with other concerns, Canadians are held to
be less conscious of class distinctions and less likely as a result to
view the world from a class perspective. Certainly, there is little
evidence that class considerations rank very high among the concerns of Candian citizens. When asked in 1974 if they ever
thought of themselves as belonging to a social class, more than
half of a national sample said no.[3]

Nor do class distinctions appear to influence the pattern of
party voting in Canada. In a well known study of the relationships between social class and voting in the Anglo-American
democracies during the 1940s and 1950s Alford concluded that
the level of class voting in Canada was considerably lower than
in Britain, Australia, or even the United States. Alford predicted
that the importance of class in Canada would increase as the nation became increasingly industrialized, but the evidence to date
does not support his expectation. Surveys of voting behaviour in
the 1965, 1968, and 1974 national elections demonstrate convincingly that social class remains, at best, a very weak determinant of voter choice in Canada.[4]

Although class and occupation appear to have little bearing
on the *direction* of the vote in Canada, the evidence regarding
their influences on the *frequency* and *intensity* of participation is
less conclusive. Not only has less consideration been given these
relationships but it is also frequently difficult to evaluate the
evidence which is available. This difficulty stems, in large part,
from the fact that research on political behaviour in Canada has
focused almost exclusively on voting, the relevance of social
class to which is problematic given the absence of political parties and candidates with well developed social-class orientations.
Moreover, research has been hampered by the difficulty of com-

paring the results of studies using different measures of social class and status. Where one approach identifies social status "objectively" using occupation as the primary indication of an individual's position in the social hierarchy, another defines social class "subjectively", assigning individuals to the class, if any, with which they identify psychologically.

Although slightly fewer than half of those interviewed in the 1974 national election study said they were members of a social class, virtually everyone was willing, when pressed on the issue, to indicate a preference for a social class however remote and politically irrelevant they considered those loyalties to be. Among those citizens who were conscious of class distinctions, fully 55 per cent said they were members of the middle class, 12 per cent identified with the upper or upper-middle classes, and a third said they were working or lower class. In contrast, those who were less attuned to class differences were only half as likely to identify with the upper classes, and were substantially more likely to be members of the working or lower classes. In other words, only about half of the members of the Canadian electorate are aware of social class distinctions and upper-middle- and upper-class citizens are substantially over-represented in this group.

The over-representation of upper- and upper-middle class interests is reinforced by the higher participation rates characteristic of the members of these groups. Among those who were conscious of class distinctions, members of the higher classes were marginally more likely to vote but substantially more likely to participate in political campaigns and to communicate directly with public officials (Table 5:1A). They also were more than twice as likely as lower- and working-class members to take part in groups concerned with community affairs. Differences between the lower classes and middle-class citizens were less pronounced (although consistent with the general patterns) indicating that the critical class distinction is the one between the small group of upper- and upper-middle class citizens and everyone else. Even when those who were less conscious of class distinctions are included in the analysis (Table 5:1B), the upper and upper-middle classes were found to participate substantially more in all four political activities; middle-

Table 5:1 THE EXTENT OF POLITICAL PARTICIPATION
BY PERCEIVED SOCIAL CLASS
(per cent)

A. Class-Conscious Citizens

Activity	Working and Lower	Middle	Upper and Upper-Middle
Voting	84	85	91
Campaigning	37	42	56
Contacting MPs	23	26	39
Community Activity	15	21	31
(N = *)	(181)	(294)	(57)

B. All Citizens Whether Conscious of Class Distinctions or Not

Activity	Working and Lower	Middle	Upper and Upper-Middle
Voting	81	85	90
Contacting MPs	37	42	53
Communicating	19	25	36
Community Activity	18	21	28
(N = *)	(464)	(575)	(97)

*Voting percentages are based on a total sample of 2,445. All other activities are based on a half-sample of 1,203. Ns are for the half-sample and vary slightly between activities because of differences in missing data.

class citizens were average participants; lower- and working-class citizens participated the least. Moreover, as expected, class differences in participation increase with the intensity of the activity and are almost twice as large for middle-level political activities, such as writing MPs or working in community groups, as for less intensive activities such as voting.

The occupational structure of Canada closely resembles those of most western industrialized societies. Approximately one-quarter of the population hold managerial or professional positions; another third are employed in clerical, commercial, or other lower-status, white-collar positions; a slightly larger percentage are blue-collar workers; and the rest (about seven per cent) are farmers. In Canada, differences in participation based on occupation (objective social status) follow the same general pattern as those based on subjective social class: professional and other white-collar workers tend to be more active than blue-collar workers in most aspects of the political process (Table 5:2). There are, however, two important exceptions.

First, although it is frequently argued that lower-status occupations allow insufficient flexibility in work schedules to accommodate extensive participation in activities other than voting, self-employed businessmen and professionals appear almost equally constrained in their political participation by occupational responsibilities. Despite their higher social status and more flexible schedules, businessmen and professionals are somewhat less likely than lower-status, white-collar workers to vote or participate in political campaigns and are about as likely to work in campaigns as the average blue-collar employee. Moreover, when they do participate in campaigns, businessmen and professionals frequently confine their involvement to contributing money whereas blue-collar workers contribute more of their time and energy.

Part of the reason that higher-status citizens do not accord greater emphasis to electoral activities may stem from a perception that they can achieve their political goals more effectively through other political avenues. In particular, the greater public visibility and social prestige of businessmen and professionals provides these individuals with better opportunities to achieve their political goals by by-passing the electoral process and communicating directly with public officials. Those at the top of the occupational pyramid may not even have to take the initiative in contacting public officials. Public officials frequently contact them in an attempt to secure their support in future elections. Indeed, studies of political recruitment in Canada suggest that political parties actively recruit individuals with highly

Table 5:2   THE EXTENT OF POLITICAL PARTICIPATION BY OCCUPATION
(per cent)

Activity	Farmer	Unskilled	Semi-Skilled	Skilled	Clerical	Manager	Businessmen and Professionals
Voting	82	82	84	81	90	87	87
Campaigning	39	35	41	33	41	49	38
Contacting MPs	23	21	21	22	21	28	30
Community Activity	31	18	18	19	15	22	25
(N* =)	(40)	(106)	(98)	(69)	(147)	(124)	(104)

*Voting percentages are based on a total sample of 2,445. All other activities are based on a half-sample of 1,203. Ns are for the half-sample and vary slightly between activities because of differences in missing data.

prestigious occupations to join the party and become candidates for public office.[5]

A second difference in the effects of occupational status and subjective social class is apparent in the political activities of farmers. Although farmers' lower-than-average participation in most activities is consistent with their typically modest social status, they are nearly twice as active as other citizens in community affairs. Despite the fact that opportunities for participation in many electoral activities are less numerous in rural areas than in the cities it is reasonable to speculate that farmers may be influenced to participate in community affairs by the stronger sense of community identification and loyalty that is characteristic of life in small towns and rural areas (a point developed in a subsequent section). This sense of community combined with more numerous opportunities for gladiator activities in rural areas may also account for Lipset's observation of the larger percentage of farmers holding low-level elected offices in the Prairie provinces.[6]

Political protest in Canada is associated with two different occupational strata. On the one hand, the high incidence of labour-related violence early in this century suggests that blue-collar workers and the unemployed are well represented in protest groups. Since he is relatively disadvantaged and perceives few traditional means of effective influence, the alienated worker is a prime recruit if organized and led. On the other hand, student "radicals" in the 1960s were disproportionately the sons and daughters of high-status families—academics and professionals in particular. Predominantly liberal political backgrounds combined with the leisure time of university, the support and encouragement of friends, and the catalyzing affect of an extraordinary series of events in the late 1960s provided both the basis of discontent and the opportunity for its expression.[7] Political protest in Quebec also has had divided class and occupational origins. For example, there is increasing evidence that the leaders of various nationalist and separatist movements in Quebec, including the Social Credit movement in the 1960s and 1970s, the Rassemblement pour l'Independence Nationale (the strongest wing of the independence movement in Quebec until 1967 or 1968), and more recently the Parti Québécois, were (are) disproportionately upper-status individuals, the majority of whom were businessmen, professionals, or industrial managers and less than one-quarter of whom were blue-collar workers or farmers. At the same time, however, Michael Stein reports that within the Social Credit movement, lower-status members were nearly twice as disaffected as higher-status members and expressed substantially greater willingness to participate in political protest.[8]

The strongest evidence of the political importance of occupation, however, is found in the literature on gladiator participation. Although lawyers, doctors, businessmen, and other professionals constitute fewer than ten per cent of the Canadian work force, they occupy almost three-quarters of the seats in the House of Commons and two-thirds of the offices in local party organizations. Blue-collar workers, in contrast, comprise nearly half of the population but hold fewer than ten per cent of the positions either in local parties or parliament. Farmers also are over-represented in parliament, although the farmer who succeeds in winning election to the House of Commons tends to be disproportionately wealthy, the owner of a large estate rather than a small farm.[9]

INCOME AND EDUCATION

Closely related to occupation and social class, education and income reinforce their political consequences. Of course, both are important in their own right as valued resources in the political arena. In a system where money is thought to be readily translated into votes, personal wealth provides significant advantages. Wealthy citizens not only can afford to contribute money to political campaigns (their own as well as others') but also are better able to bear the financial burdens of holding public office. Not surprisingly, therefore, the affluent are widely recruited by political parties.

What is surprising, given the emphasis placed upon limiting the importance of money in politics, is not that wealth is related to political participation but that this relationship is so weak (Table 5:3). Citizens earning in excess of $20,000 annually are more likely than less-affluent citizens to contact public officials,

Table 5:3   THE EXTENT OF POLITICAL PARTICIPATION
BY PERSONAL INCOME
(per cent)

Activity	Less than $5,000	$5,000 to $9,999	$10,000 to $14,999	$15,000 to $19,999	$20,000 +
Voting	83	84	86	85	88
Campaigning	43	35	40	41	46
Contacting MPs	20	19	25	24	33
Community Activity	22	18	22	20	21
(N* =)	(173)	(330)	(289)	(228)	(159)

*Voting percentages are based on a total sample of 2,445. All other activities are based on a half-sample of 1,203. NS are for the half-sample and vary slightly between activities because of differences in missing data.

but are only average participants in community affairs. Nor are the rich appreciably more likely to vote or participate in political campaigns than even the poorest citizens. The primary advantage of wealth is found at the upper levels of the political spectrum. It facilitates communication with political parties and public officials and increases opportunities for full-time political work, but there is little evidence that money discriminates between activists and apathetics in other areas.

Whereas money is frequently disparaged as the root of political mischief, education is typically viewed in the opposite light. An educated electorate is widely regarded as a prime requisite for stable democratic rule. Education, it is argued, not only promotes public rationality and tolerance but fosters a more active polity. The rationale is a familiar one. Education increases political awareness, interest, and information. It contributes to an appreciation of the personal relevance of political decisions, inculcates a sense of civic obligation, and broadens political attitudes and beliefs and provides them with a rational basis. Educated citizens are said to read more, remember more of what they read, and, therefore, are more sensitive to the available political messages in the environment. Moreover, education is frequently linked to opportunity. The more citizens understand about the political process and the various avenues for individual involvement, the better equipped they are to take advantage of them. Finally, education contributes to personal confidence and self-esteem, feelings observed in Chapter 4 to be readily transferred to politics. Such, at least, is the prevailing liberal theory.

The reality of education's influence on political behaviour, however, is more complex than the theory (Table 5:4). Citizens with at least some high-school education are more likely to vote than those with none, but high-school and university graduates are no more likely to participate in elections than those who attended high school but failed to graduate. Similarly, the levels of campaign activity and community involvement increase with education through the end of high school but *decline* thereafter. It is, then, the high-school graduate who is most convinced of the value of campaign and community activities. Citizens with less education, even though imbued with a strong sense of civic responsibility, are far less likely to perceive the value of individual activity and are less likely as a result to feel personally efficacious. More highly educated citizens also accept the democratic creed but are cynical about the effectiveness of participation in collective activities compared with direct personal involvement.

It is participation in the highest-level political activities (i.e., communicating with public officials, serving as a political party official, and holding public office) which is most convincingly explained by the prevailing theory. Education also is among the best predictors of political protest, although it is not clear whether this has aways been the case or is a reflection of the political discontent on university campuses in the 1960s and early 1970s.

ETHNICITY, LANGUAGE, AND RELIGION

Few aspects of the Canadian political culture have been as thoroughly discussed as the absence of a national identity and the tenacity with which ethnic and regional cultures have resisted

Table 5:4   THE EXTENT OF POLITICAL PARTICIPATION
BY EDUCATIONAL ACHIEVEMENT
(per cent)

Activity	Grades 0 – 9	Some High School	High School Graduate	Some College or Higher Education	College Graduate
Voting	80	86	87	90	86
Campaigning	35	40	48	44	42
Contacting MPS	19	25	26	27	32
Community Activity	18	20	24	21	22
(N* =)	(318)	(328)	(194)	(147)	(216)

*Voting percentages are based on a total sample of 2,445. All other activities are based on a half-sample of 1,203. NS are for the half-sample and vary slightly between activities because of differences in missing data.

assimilation. Arising out of the early conquest of one cultural fragment by another and the subsequent onslaught of successive waves of immigration from diverse areas of the world, ethnic divisions in Canada have been reinforced by group differences in language, religion, lifestyle, and philosophy and by regional differences in wealth, industrialization, and urbanization. Given also the innundation of many parts of Canada by U.S. media and culture, it is no wonder that ethnic loyalties have persisted or that attempts to promote an over-riding Canadian national identity have proven largely unsuccessful.

Although Canadian society is a mosaic of many and diverse ethnic cultures, the importance of ethnicity is most apparent in the continuing deep divisions between French and English Canada. Compared to other Anglo-American societies, the United States in particular, the Canadian political culture is frequently characterized as being both highly elitist and deferential toward authority—traits which contribute to what has been described as Canada's "quasi-participant" or "spectator" political culture. Although characteristic of Canada as a whole, these traits are particularly evident in French Canada whose history and religion have contributed to what one authority describes as "a practically spontaneous acceptance of authority and hierarchy in the family, in society, and the state. French Canadians like to be ruled."[11]

Whether French Canadians do like to be ruled (especially by English bosses) is highly problematic. However, substantial evidence does exist to support Pierre Trudeau's more moderate assessment—issued before he entered public office—that Quebec's cultural and political heritage prejudiced the development of democratic attitudes and poorly equipped French Canadians for the responsibilities of democratic citizenship.[12]

Consistent with Trudeau's argument, the data from the 1974 national election survey indicate that French Canadians are less active in most political activities at the national level than citizens with Anglo-Celtic backgrounds (Table 5:5). French-Canadian respondents were less likely to vote in federal elections, communicate with MPs, or work with others to solve community problems at the national level. However, French Canadians were more likely to participate in national political campaigns and were more active in most provincial-level political activities as well (data for the latter not shown).

However, rather than confirming Trudeau's assessment of the weakness of the French-Canadian commitment to democratic norms, these observations suggest that the extent of French-Canadian participation depends in part on the political context. Given the opportunity to take part in a distinctly French-Canadian context, French-Canadian citizens appear to be as active as the members of any other ethnic group. Although such opportunities are numerous at the provincial level, they are comparatively rare in national politics. The federal structure of the party system is an exception and provides one of the few substantial avenues for French-Canadian participation in national political institutions with distinctively French-Canadian perspectives.

Another reason for the French Canadians' relative emphasis on participation in political campaigns may be the greater appeal which party patronage traditionally has held for the least affluent and assimilated members of society. Although the continuing rise in standards of living and growth of the welfare

Table 5:5   THE EXTENT OF POLITICAL PARTICIPATION
BY ETHNIC ORIGIN
(per cent)

Activity	British	French	Other European	Asian, Native Other
Voting	88	82	85	81
Campaigning	38	43	43	41
Contacting MPs	26	19	26	25
Community Activity	26	15	17	24
(N* =)	(536)	(267)	(186)	(142)

*Voting percentages are based on a total sample of 2,445. All other activities are based on a half-sample of 1,203. NS are for the half-sample and vary slightly between activities because of differences in missing data.

state have reduced the importance of traditional forms of patronage, political parties still control substantial material resources with which to reward party faithful.[13] Perhaps more importantly, parties also provide a sense of belonging to less-assimilated citizens in what otherwise may seem to be an alien society. That other European ethnic groups share the French-Canadian enthusiasm for campaign work supports this explanation. On the other hand, however, political parties have less direct control over the types of political patronage sought by wealthier citizens, i.e., government contracts, tax relief, or the construction of roads and schools. These goals are often more effectively pursued through organized community action or direct communication with public officials—activities dominated, not surprisingly, by the better educated, affluent, and assimilated.

Gladiator participation in Canada also is dominated by members of the older and established "charter" groups. Although the Liberal party has dominated federal politics since the Second World War and receives a disproportionate share of its support from French-Canadian and Central European ethnic groups, membership in the House of Commons continues to reflect the over-representation of Canadians of Anglo-Celtic and Northern European descent.[14] Political protest, in contrast, is most prevalent among the least-assimilated groups in society as is evident from the record of French-Canadian protest during the 1960s, from the activities of radical segments of groups such as the Doukhobors in British Columbia, and from the ethnic composition of labour protests over the first half of this century.

Closely related to ethnicity, linguistic and religious differences have similar political consequences. English-speaking citizens are more likely to vote, participate in community affairs, and write to public officials, but Francophone and bilingual citizens play a more active role in political campaigns. Protestants are more likely to vote, write to public officials, and participate in community affairs, but Catholics are more deeply involved in political campaigns. Jews, however, are clearly the religious political elite. Although average participants in elections and community affairs, Jews are more likely to contact public officials and to participate in political campaigns than any other group. (Nearly three-quarters of the Jewish respondents in 1974 reported participating in the campaign.) Students from Jewish families also were disproportionately active in the college protests of the 1960s.

AGE, SEX, AND COMMUNITY

Although the Age of Majority Act lowered the federal voting age to eighteen and increased the number of eligible voters by more than one million, conventional wisdom has tended to discount its political significance. The explanation usually advanced is that newly enfranchised voters, the young in particular, mime their elders and are slow to exercise independent political rights. More generally, it is argued, the relationship between age and participation is curvilinear: participation tends to be lowest among the young, increasing through middle age, and declining again in later years. According to Lester Milbrath,

there are three intervening variables relating age to participation: integration with the community, the availability of blocks of leisure time, and good health. Integration . . .

develops with marriage, job responsibility, and acquiring a family; thus, participation rises gradually with advancing age . . . . Young children and other confinements delay the full opportunity for participation, especially for young mothers. Finally, in the twilight years, physical infirmities probably account for most of the decline in participation.[15]

More than the experience of growing old, age-related variations in behaviour also reflect generational differences in social background and historical circumstance.[16] Although the elderly usually participate less because they have lower levels of education, and the young because of the unsettling experiences of leaving home, getting married, and beginning work, particular generations may deviate from this pattern if the environment in which they grew up was unusually politicized.

In Canada, the pattern of activity characteristic of citizens *over the age of twenty-one* closely resembles the curvilinear model (Table 5:6). Voting, campaigning, and community involvement are generally lowest among those in the 21-35 group, highest among those in the 36-50 group, and lower again among the older generations. Although differences in participation among citizens over thirty-five are somewhat reduced when education and social status are controlled, the gap between the young and the middle-aged increases when these background factors are considered. However, idiosyncratic generational effects are most apparent among the age group between eighteen and twenty-one. Although these youngest citizens are less likely than their elders to participate in community affairs or to communicate with public officials, they are among the most active voters and campaign participants. Growing up in a period of relative political turmoil, the children of the sixties apparently were exposed to more intense political experiences than older generations. That the political energy of the young is expended largely on electoral activities is probably a function of opportunity in that citizens under twenty-one have relatively more time than many of their elders to devote to political campaigns but have few opportunities to run for political office and are insufficiently integrated into the community to be active participants in community affairs.

Table 5:6   THE EXTENT OF POLITICAL PARTICIPATION BY AGE
(per cent)

Activity	18 – 21	22 – 35	36 – 50	51 – 65	66 +
Voting	86	82	86	87	85
Campaigning	43	36	45	40	38
Contacting MPs	14	26	26	24	20
Community Activity	13	16	26	21	20
(N* =)	(127)	(362)	(332)	(249)	(128)

*Voting percentages are based on a total sample of 2,445. All other activities are based on a half-sample of 1,203. NS are for the half-sample and vary slightly between activities because of differences in missing data.

If politics traditionally has been the preserve of the middle-aged, it has been even more a game for men. Although sex differences are most obvious at the upper levels of politics (where fewer than five per cent of all MPs and twenty per cent of local party officials are women), they exist to a lesser degree in virtually every type of political activity. Women are slightly less likely to vote than men (84 *versus* 88 per cent); they are less active in political campaigns and community activities (39 and 19 per cent respectively for women *versus* 42 and 23 per cent for men) despite the fact that women, housewives in particular, are reported to have more flexible schedules if not more leisure time; and they are substantially less likely to communicate with public officials (20 *versus* 28 per cent). Two explanations are usually offered: first, that women bear disproportionate responsibilities for maintaining the home and rearing the family and thus have fewer, not greater, opportunities for participation and, second, that they are socialized into a set of roles emphasizing women's domestic obligations and deprecating their abilities to compete equally with men. This second factor, it is argued, diminishes their self-esteem and hinders the development of women's feelings of personal competence and political efficacy.

Although there is some evidence that sex differences in participation are being eroded by the combined effects of a declining birth rate, the success of the women's liberation movement, and the tendency of increasing numbers of women to pursue independent careers, it is still too early to tell what the political results of these changes will be. What is apparent, however, is that changes are occurring. Few politicians today would publicly defend the point of view expressed twenty years ago by a noted political scientist that,

> . . . working girls and career women, and women who insistently serve the community in volunteer capacities, and women with extracurricular interests of an absorbing kind are often borrowing their time and attention and capacity for relaxed play and love from their children to whom it rightfully belongs.[17]

Women may not have achieved political equality, but they clearly "have come a long way".

The importance of the influence of behaviour exerted by one's community has been emphasized at several points. Where one resides is closely related not only to occupation, social status, income, ethnicity, and the host of other sociological attributes discussed in this chapter, but also to many of the psychological and personality traits catalogued in Chapter 4. Among the more critical aspects of the community is size. One theory, the urbanization thesis, describes cities as the cultural, commercial, and political centres of society, providing their residents greater opportunities and stronger motivation for political action than are characteristic of rural areas.[18] Urban environments, it is argued, facilitate mass communication, provide a wider range of educational opportunities, increase ethnic and religious integration, and enhance both the scope and sophistication of individual attitudes. Rural environments, according to this view, are largely peripheral to the political system. They are devoid of cultural stimulation and political opportunity and characterized by parochial political values.

The urbanization thesis, however, has never enjoyed universal acceptance. An opposing view celebrates the virtues of rural life and indicts the cities for destroying the human spirit and promoting alienation. The contemporary version of this thesis praises modern means of transportation and communication for extending the advantages of urban life to the residents of smaller towns and farms without subjecting rural dwellers to the depersonalizing experiences of overcrowding, crime, and urban squalor. Acknowledging that opportunities for certain forms of collective action remain relatively less available outside the metropolitan centres, the greater sense of community shared by residents of rural areas is seen as ample compensation.

The evidence from 1974 provides some support for both theories and indicates the relationship between urbanization and participation is generally curvilinear (Table 5:7). Excluding residents of rural towns and farms, cities are the hubs of political activity. Although citizens from the largest cities and suburbs are slightly less active in community affairs than residents in smaller cities, large-city and suburban dwellers are slightly more likely to vote and substantially more active in gladiator activities and political protests. Suburban dwellers also are more active in political campaigns.

It is the rural villager and farmer, however, who live the most active political lives. Although required to travel greater distances to the polls, farmers are among the most consistent voters in Canada. They are average participants in political campaigns despite fewer opportunities. And they communicate with public officials more frequently than most. Even more dramatically farmers and rural villagers are twice as active as other citizens in community affairs—clear evidence, we believe, of their greater sense of community. Farmers also are disproportionately likely to hold parliamentary or other public offices—although the Canadian Cincinnatus is recruited from a country estate more often than a farm.[19]

TOWARDS A MULITVARIATE EXPLANATION OF PARTICIPATION

Fundamental to understanding the causes of political participation in Canada is the assumption, developed in the introduction to Chapter 4, that political motivations are the final link in a complex chain of individual attitudes and experiences anchored in childhood and extending across the life-cycle. Although the evidence reviewed in chapters 4 and 5 is compati-

Table 5:7 THE EXTENT OF POLITICAL PARTICIPATION
BY SIZE OF COMMUNITY
(per cent)

Activity	Cities 500,000+	Suburbs 500,000=	Cities 30,000-500,000	Towns 1,000-30,000	Rural/Farm
Voting	86	87	83	84	86
Campaigning	39	43	41	35	41
Contacting MPS	24	21	23	24	26
Community Activity	13	15	17	25	31
(N* =)	(193)	(256)	(298)	(181)	(277)

*Voting percentages are based on a total sample of 2,445. All other activities are based on a half-sample of 1,203. NS are for the half-sample and vary slightly between activities because of differences in missing data.

ble with this assumption, bivariate analyses are insufficient to confirm what is explicitly a multivariate explanation.

In an earlier and more sophisticated examination of the causes of voting, campaigning, and party work in Canada, Mishler constructed a mulitvariate model using many of the same psychological and sociological variables discussed in this and the previous chapter.[20] An outline of the model is reconstructed in Figure 5:1. Consistent with the theory thus far developed, political participation is conceptualized in the model as a direct consequence of adult political attitudes (or motivations) tempered by opportunity, and as an indirect result both of early life and adult experiences and of political attitudes acquired during childhood and adolescence. Adult political attitudes, however, are the critical link in the model. Although sociological variables have important consequences, their impact on participation is held to be indirect and mediated through the intervening effects of current motivations. Similarly, consistent with a large body of literature on political socialization (discussed at length in Chapter 6), political attitudes acquired early in life also are assumed to influence adult behaviour indirectly in

Figure 5:1   A MODEL OF THE DETERMINANTS OF POLITICAL PARTICIPATION IN CANADA*

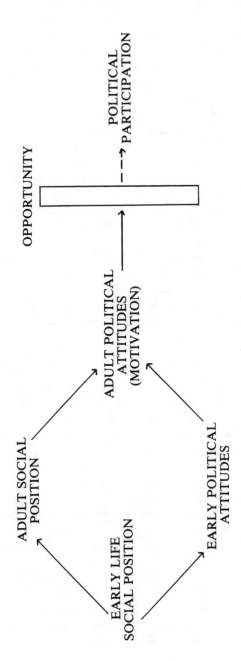

*Adapted from William Mishler, "Political Participation and the Process of Political Socialization in Canada'', Ph.D. Thesis, Duke University, 1972.

so far as they either become an integral part of the adult personality or condition the subsequent development of other political attitudes through a psychological process known as selective perception. Early-life experiences stand in the same relationship to early political attitudes in the model as adult experiences stand to adult motivations. They are held to be two steps removed from behaviour and influence participation to the extent that citizens' social positions remain relatively stable between generations or early political experiences influence the development of early and persistent political attitudes.

Tests of the model with data collected in two Canadian cities, provided support for these assumptions. Consistent with their positions in the model, Mishler found that current attitudes consistently exhibited the strongest relationships with the several measures of participation whereas the early-life-experience variables manifested the weakest correlations. More importantly, although virtually all of the social position and early political-attitude variables were strongly related to political activity, these relationships were substantially attenuated when the effects of adult political attitudes were controlled.

THE QUESTION OF QUALITY

The accumulated evidence from chapters 4 and 5 supports the fundamental premise that political motivations are extensions of individual personalities whose origins can be traced, in turn, to social, economic, and political experience.[21] Far from being an inevitable consequence of man's inherent apathy, the oligarchic structure of political activity in Canada appears to be learned—the result of a combination of individual experiences and historical events. However, before examining the process of political learning in greater detail, consideration must be given to another aspect of the democratic debate, specifically to what has been called the question of quality.

Although a politically active population is central to classical democratic theory, participation is only one of several requirements. Citizens also are expected to be well informed, rational, and tolerant. As was noted in Chapter 1, contemporary opposition to increasing direct participation stems from elitists' observations that few citizens possess these qualities and their fears that increased participation would, as a consequence, jeopardize the quality of democratic life. Critics of the elitists counter that form and substance are inseparable. Although they acknowledge the quality of public opinion is low, they place the blame on the widespread sense of alienation born of inadequate opportunities for effective participation at work, in the family, and at school, as well as in politics. Increasing participation in these other areas, in their view, would simultaneously enhance both the quality and the quantity of political activity.

Although it is extremely difficult to establish cause and effect with the data and methods available in the social sciences, the evidence from the preceding chapters lends evidence to the contemporary democratic view. Participants in most activities (all but political protest) are less alienated than non-participants. Political activists are characterized by a greater sense of political competence, efficacy, and trust, and they tend to be better educated, better informed about politics and public policy, and more consistent in their political attitudes and behaviour. Although little evidence exists on the relationship between democratic values and participation in Canada, research in other nations—principally the United States—comfirms that prejudice, dogmatism, and a willingness to embrace authoritarian values also are most prevalent among those least active in politics.[22]

Some of the strongest evidence of the relationship between the quality and quantity of *political* participation on the one hand and opportunities for *non-political* participation on the other is reported by the elitists. Almond and Verba hypothesize, for example, that participation in non-political organizations "may be considered training for the performance of political roles". Although emphasizing the relationship is by no means unambiguous and is at least partially contingent on education, they conclude that "if an individual has had the opportunity to participate in the family, in school, or at work, he is more likely than someone who did not have the same opportunities to consider himself competent to influence government."[23] Moreover, they found the impact of non-political opportunities to be cumulative. Citizens who enjoyed consistent opportunities for participation in non-political areas were most likely of all to carry a generalized sense of personal competence into the political arena.

Elaborating on the importance of job participation, in particular, Carole Pateman concludes from a survey of the recent literature that even limited worker participation may be sufficient to increase political interest and efficacy, to promote tolerance and integration (thereby reinforcing co-operation and stability), and to foster the development of democratic personalities.[24] The consequences of participation will be considered at greater length in Chapter 7. However, it appears from this preliminary survey that the quality of participation varies directly with its practice. Rather than threatening the quality of democratic life, increased participation both whets the political appetite and educates the palate.

SUMMARY

Political activists in Canada are a diverse group. They are motivated by a variety of concerns and drawn from every segment of society. Nevertheless, it is apparent that certain social and economic experiences contribute disproportionately to the development of political personalities. Motivations are learned and certain backgrounds provide stronger political educations. But how is experience translated into behaviour? What is the shape of the political learning process in Canada? And how can this process be harnessed for the expansion of democratic citizenship? These are the questions to which we now turn.

NOTES

1. The most thorough review of the effects of socio-economic background on participation remains Robert Lane's classic, *Political Life* (New York, 1959), pp. 187-275. See for a more recent review of the literature, Lester Milbrath and M. L. Goal, *Political Participation*, rev. ed. (Chicago, 1977). On Canada, see Mildred A. Schwartz, "Canadian Voting Behavior", in Richard Rose, ed., *Electoral Behavior* (New York, 1974), pp. 543-617; David J. Elkins and Donald E. Blake, "Voting Research in Canada: Problems and Prospects", *Canadian Journal of Political Science*, Vol. 8 (June 1975), pp. 313-25; and John Terry and Richard Schultz, "Canadian

Electoral Behaviour: A Propositional Inventory", in O. M. Kruhlak, ed., *The Canadian Political Process* (Toronto, 1973), pp. 248-85.

2. See, for example, Robert R. Alford, *Party and Society: The Anglo-American Democracies* (Chicago, 1963); Alford, "Class Voting in the Anglo-American Political Systems", in S. M. Lipset and S. Rokkan, eds., *Party Systems and Voter Alignments* (New York, 1967), pp. 65-93; and John Wilson, "Politics and Social Class in Canada: The Case of Waterloo South", *Canadian Journal of Political Science*, Vol. 1 (September 1968), pp. 288-309. Among the better treatments of the dissenting view is John Porter, *The Vertical Mosaic* (Toronto, 1965); and more recently, Nelson Wiseman and K. W. Taylor, "Ethnic *vs.* Class Voting: The Case of Winnipeg, 1945", *Canadian Journal of Political Science*, Vol. 7 (June 1974), pp. 314-28. Increasing evidence is being marshalled to support the proposition that the importance of class and social status varies by region. See Richard Simeon and David J. Elkins, "Regional Political Cultures in Canada", *Canadian Journal of Political Science*, Vol. 7 (September 1974), pp. 397-437.

3. Unless otherwise indicated, the data used in this chapter are from the 1974 Canadian National Election Study.

4. Harold D. Clarke, *et al., Political Choice in Canada* (Toronto, 1979), Chapter 4.

5. See, for example, William Mishler, "Nominating Attractive Candidates for Parliament", *Legislative Studies Quarterly* (November 1978); see also, Allan Kornberg, Harold Clarke, and George Watson, "Toward a Model of Parliamentary Recruitment in Canada", in Allan Kornberg, *Legislatures in Comparative Perspective* (New York, 1973), pp. 250-81.

6. Seymore Martin Lipset, *Agrarian Socialism* (Berkeley, 1950), Chapter 10.

7. Richard Flacks, "The Liberated Generation: An Exploration of the Roots of Student Protest", *Journal of Social Issues*, Vol. 23 (1967), pp. 52-75; and Susan Welch, "Dimensions of Political Participation in a Canadian Sample", *Canadian Journal of Political Science,* Vol. 8 (December 1975), Table IV.

8. Michael Stein, *The Dynamics of Right-Wing Protest: A Political Analysis of Social Credit in Quebec* (Toronto, 1973), chapters 4 and 5.

9. Harold D. Clarke, Richard G. Price, and Robert Krause, "Backbenchers", in David J. Bellamy, Jon H. Pammett, and Donald C. Rowat, eds., *The Provincial Political Systems* (Toronto, 1976), pp. 216-19; Allan Kornberg, "Parliament in Canadian Society", in Allan Kornberg and Lloyd D. Musolf, eds., *Legislatures in Developmental Perspective* (Durham, N.C., 1970), pp. 55-128; and Allan Kornberg, Joel Smith, and David Bromley, "Some Differences in the Political Socialization Patterns of Canadian and

American Party Officials: A Preliminary Report", *Canadian Journal of Political Science*, Vol. 2 (March 1969), p. 73.

10. See for example, Porter, *The Vertical Mosaic*, Chapter 3. Simeon and Elkins, "Regional Political Cultures in Canada", *passim*; John Wilson, "The Canadian Political Cultures: Toward a Redefinition of the Nature of Canadian Political Cultures", *Canadian Journal of Political Science*, Vol. 7 (September 1974), pp. 438-83; and Mildred A. Schwartz, *Politics and Territory: The Sociology of Regional Persistence in Canada* (Montreal, 1973). An excellent summary of the roots of contemporary ethnic cleavages in Canada is Kenneth O. McRae, "The Structure of Canadian History", in Louis Hartz, ed., *The Founding of New Societies* (New York, 1964).

11. Esdras Minville, *L'Avenir de Notre Bourgeoisie*, as cited in Robert Presthus, *Elite Accommodation in Canadian Politics* (Toronto, 1973), p. 49.

12. "Some Obstacles to Democracy in Quebec", *Canadian Journal of Economics and Political Science*, Vol. 24 (August 1958), pp. 297-311.

13. On the continuing importance of patronage see S. J. R. Noel, "Leadership and Clientelism", in Bellamy, Pammett, and Rowat, *The Provincial Political Systems*, pp. 197-213. See also, Jonathan Manthorpe, *The Power and the Tories* (Toronto, 1974).

14. Although only slightly under-represented numerically in parliament, French Canadians are substantially under-represented in terms of the influence ascribed to French-Canadian MPs. See in this regard, Kornberg and Mishler, *Influence in Parliament*, Chapter III.

15. Milbrath and Goal, *Political Participation*, p. 135.

16. See, for example, James E. Curtis and Ronald D. Lambert, "Voting, Election Interest, and Age: National Findings for English and French Canadians", *Canadian Journal of Political Science*, Vol. 9 (June 1976), pp. 293-307, and Norman H. Nie, Sidney Verba, and Jae-on Kim, "Political Participation Through the Life Cycle", *Comparative Politics* (April 1974), pp. 319-40.

17. Lane, *Political Life*, p. 355.

18. The best-known advocates of this view are Karl Deutsch, "Social Mobilization and Political Development", *American Political Science Review*, Vol. 55 (September 1961), pp. 493-514; and Daniel Lerner, *The Passing of Traditional Society* (Glencoe, 1960). For evidence disputing this theory see Norman Nie, G. Bingham Powell, and Kenneth Prewitt, "Social Structure and Political Participation, Part I", *American Political Science Review*, Vol. 63 (June 1969), pp. 361-78.

19. See, for example, Roman March, "An Empirical Test of M. Ostragorskei's Theory of Political Evaluation in a British Parliamentary System", Ph.D. Thesis, Indiana University, 1967. See also Kornberg, "Parliament in Canadian Society", pp. 84-92.

20. William Mishler, "Political Participation and the Process of Political Socialization in Canada", Ph.D. Thesis, Duke University, 1972, chapters 4 and 5.
21. In addition to the effects of individual experience, substantial evidence has been marshalled regarding the influence on both personality and behaviour of genetic and biochemical factors. Indeed it has been estimated by one source that basic traits such as intelligence may be as much as eighty per cent determined by genetic inheritance. Several have noted the possibility, as well, of manipulating political behaviour through the selective administration of various drugs and chemicals. Not surprisingly, such evidence as has been produced in these regards has been strongly challenged on both normative and empirical grounds. See, for an introduction to these debates, Albert Somit, "Towards a More Biologically Oriented Political Science: Ethnology and Psychopharmacology", *Midwest Journal of Political Science*, Vol. 12 (August 1968), pp. 550-67; Dean Jaros, "Biochemical Desocialization: Depressants and Political Behavior", *Midwest Journal of Political Science*, Vol. 16 (February 1972), pp. 1-22; and A. R. Jensen, *et al., Environment, Heredity, and Intelligence* (Cambridge, 1969).
22. See, in particular, Herbert McClosky, Paul J. Hoffman, and Rosemary O'Hara, "Issue Conflict and Consensus Among Party Leaders and Followers", *American Political Science Review*, Vol. 54 (June 1960), pp. 406-77; Herbert McClosky, "Consensus and Ideology in American Politics", *American Political Science Review*, Vol. 58 (June 1964), pp. 361-82; Samuel Stouffer, *Communism, Conformity and Civil Liberties* (New York, 1966); and William Kornhouser, *The Politics of Mass Society* (New York, 1959).
23. *The Civic Culture* (Boston, 1965), pp. 271 and 300; a similar argument can be constructed from the evidence reported in Jon H. Pammett, "Adolescent Political Activity as a Learning Experience: The Action-Trudeau Campaign of 1968", in Jon H. Pammett and Michael S. Whittington, eds., *Foundations of Political Culture* (Toronto, 1976), pp. 160-94.
24. *Participation and Democratic Theory* (London, 1970), chapters IV and V. An impressionistic attempt to apply similar arguments to worker participation in Canada is H. B. Wilson's, *Democracy and the Workplace* (Montreal, 1974), esp. Chapter 3.

6.　　　　Learning to
　　　　　Participate

Political attitudes and behaviour are learned. The political apathy and inactivity characteristic of large segments of the Canadian public are not intrinsic to man's basic nature; they are neither inevitable nor immutable. The decision to participate in or abstain from politics is, to a substantial degree, a conditioned response to the political environment predicated upon a set of individual attitudes acquired and nurtured throughout life. Moreover, because political behaviour is learned, knowledge of the learning process provides opportunities for improving political learning and thereby increasing both the extent of political participation and the quality of democratic citizenship.

The idea of improving citizenship through political education is not new. From earliest times, political philosophers and public officials have recognized a need for some form of citizenship training, political education, or social engineering to establish a basis for social and political order—a need which Whiting and Child describe graphically:

> In all societies the helpless infant feeding at his mother's breast, . . . freely evacuating the waste products, exploring his genitals, biting and kicking at will, must be changed into a responsible adult obeying the rules of society.[1]

No less than other regimes, democratic government presupposes public consensus on fundamental values. Although warning against the tyranny of socialized habit, John Stuart Mill insisted that citizenship be contingent upon education, prohibiting the right to participate to those in society whom he considered insufficiently "prepared" for self government. However, Mill believed that sanctions should not be necessary.

He argued that society has other means to bring "its weakest members up to its ordinary standard of rational conduct. . . . Society has had absolute power over them during all the early portion of their existence; it has had the whole period of childhood and nonage in which to try whether it could make them capable of rational conduct in life."[2] Rousseau was even more emphatic. He argued that citizens must be "taught what it is they will" and forced, through proper education, to be free.

Although the concept of political education dates from antiquity, social scientists only recently have begun to examine systematically the processes by which political attitudes and behaviour are acquired. As a consequence, even the definition of the concept remains subject to dispute. Early definitions of political education (or political socialization as it is frequently called), stressed that the process involves the transmission from one generation to the next of "political norms and behaviours acceptable to the ongoing political system".[3] However, responding to criticism of the conservative bias inherent in this definition with its emphasis on "system maintenance", recent definitions have promoted a broader view that political socialization includes "those developmental processes through which persons acquire political orientations and behaviour" whether acceptable to the current political system or not.[4] We will treat political socialization in the latter sense as the study of political learning—a multifaceted discipline concerned, as Greenstein describes it, with the study of "who learns what from whom under what circumstances and with what effects".[5] This chapter examines the content and process of political learning—the questions of who, what, from whom, and under what circumstances. Chapter 7 addresses the question of consequences.

WHO LEARNS WHAT?

In one sense, the answers to the questions, who learns and what is learned, are implicit in the discussions in chapters 4 and 5 of the psychological and social correlates of political participation. Those who are most politically active are wealthy, middle-aged males with extensive formal educations and high-status occupations. These people are among the most likely to have acquired an appreciation of the personal relevance of political decisions, a sense of political efficacy, substantial information about politics and public policy, a strong sense of community, and a high level of political interest.

In a more fundamental sense, however, everyone may be said to learn about politics. Inactivity and the attitudes associated with it are learned as much as are the attitudes underlying the most intensive forms of political action. Everyone learns; it is what and how they learn which varies and explains differences in political behaviour.

BASIC ORIENTATIONS

The process of political learning starts early and continues at an uneven pace throughout life. Beginning in childhood (some say *in utero*), citizens gradually acquire a broad range of values, emotions, and beliefs about a variety of political objects including the nation, its political institutions and laws, its leaders and policies, and the role of the individual within the political process.

One of the earliest and most fundamental orientations which children learn is a sense of patriotism, or "us *versus* them". The perception of belonging to a community and of loyalty to its symbols often develops before the child is of school age. In one study, conducted before the Maple Leaf was adopted as the national flag, primary-school children were shown the flags of twenty nations and asked to select one they liked best. Three-quarters of the students in Grade 1 selected one of the two Canadian flags—the Union Jack and the Red Ensign. The flag of the United States was also favoured, but those of other, more alien nations or organizations such as the Soviet Union and the United Nations, were not.[6]

Political orientations, like patriotism, which develop early tend to have an emotional basis and, thus, are highly resistant to change. Only strong and repeated provocations cause them to be re-evaluated. Among Indians in Cape Breton, for example, even the experience of being members of a severely disadvantaged minority has had little effect on their loyalties to Canada. Although slightly less affectionate toward Canada than white

Cape Breton children of the same age, nearly half of the Indian youth surveyed in one study thought "Canada [to be] the best country in the world". Fewer than fifteen per cent dissented.[7]

As a child matures his awareness of political institutions widens. In a study of adolescents in grades 4-9, Pammett and Whittington report that fewer than twenty per cent of the youngest students were able to identify as many as half of a group of prominent political officials ranging from the prime minister to the mayor. This figure increased to ninety per cent among the oldest group of students. Moreover, when asked to compare the political power exercised in Canada by the Queen, the governor general, and the prime minister, nearly two-thirds of the students in Grade 4 said the Queen was most powerful, and fewer than 30 per cent chose the prime minister. By Grade 9, however, these proportions were reversed.[8]

Although Canadian youth generally recognize and admire the country's political symbols and institutions, their loyalties are not as strong as those exhibited by students in the United States. Inundated by American media and culture, Canadian children initially find it difficult to distinguish between politics in Canada and the United States. The most dramatic example occurs in a study reporting that more than fifteen per cent of the students in Grade 2 thought that Richard Nixon was the prime minister of Canada and twelve per cent said Pierre Trudeau was president of the United States. Older students were better informed but continued to display remarkable affection for American institutions and leaders. As one would expect, most adolescents felt closer to the Queen and prime minister than to the president. Nevertheless, in 1971, one student in six preferred the president to the Queen and one in four preferred the president—then, Richard Nixon—to Prime Minister Trudeau. Even more remarkable, nearly a quarter of the students expressed greater confidence in the president than the Queen and more than one-third thought President Nixon "more likely to make the right decisions" than Prime Minister Trudeau.[9]

The influence of the United States declines as students mature. However, national symbols face increasing competition from local and provincial symbols for the "hearts and minds" of Canadian youth. When students in Cape Breton were asked, for example, whether they felt greater pride in Canada, Nova Scotia, or Cape Breton, more than 60 per cent of the nine- and ten-year-olds but fewer than half of those seventeen to nineteen years old chose Canada. However, older students were twice as likely as the younger group to select Cape Breton.[10]

The supremacy of provincial loyalties seems to be firmly established by the end of secondary school. A majority of Anglophone students (Grades 11 and 12) in Manitoba and Ontario, no less than Francophone students in Quebec, believe their interests are best served by provincial government.[11] Only English-speakers in Quebec express greater confidence in the federal administration and these students are ambivalent about their choice.

Not surprisingly, it is the Francophone youth of Quebec whose national loyalties are most strained. When asked in 1968 how they preferred to think of themselves, seven out of ten English-speaking students—whether in Manitoba, Ontario, or Quebec—replied simply, "Canadian." Only twenty per cent of the Francophone Quebeckers accepted this label without adding significant qualifications. Nor do English- and French-speaking students grow up believing they have much in common. Nearly forty per cent of the Anglophones and seventy per cent of the Francophones considered members of the other linguistic group "as being like foreign people".[12] Since so many Canadians learn early to view large numbers of fellow citizens as aliens, it is not surprising they show a strong sense of alienation as adults.

Neither is it surprising that support for separatist and independence movements in Canada has steadily increased in recent years, especially among young Francophone citizens in Quebec. Almost a decade before the victory of the Parti Québécois in 1976 signalled the coming of age of the Quebec separatist and independence movements, Johnstone and Lamy, in separate studies, found strong evidence of increasing polarization in the political attitudes and loyalties of French- and English-Canadian youth.[13] In addition to confirming, for example, that provincial loyalties increase with age among both Anglophone and Francophone youth, Johnstone observed a nearly three-fold increase in French-Canadian disaffection for the federal government between individuals who were 13 and 14 years old in 1965 and those who were 19 and 20. On other important issues as well, Johnstone found that, "Members of the two cultures . . . enter adulthood a good deal further apart in their views . . . than they were when they entered adolescence."[14]

More significantly, Lamy reports that sympathy for Quebec separatism and independence increased dramatically between members of the youngest (11-13) and oldest (17-20) cohorts of French-Canadian youth in his 1968 survey while among English-Canadian youth the pattern was one of increasing antipathy toward both separatism and independence for Quebec. According to Lamy, these tendencies were foreboding of "significant cleavages between French and English Canadians on concepts which seem fundamental to the existence and stability of the present Canadian system. . . . Political socialization in Canada, then, seems to be for young French and English Canadians a process of socialization into discord. . . ."[15]

The victory of the Parti Québécois in 1976 appears to validate these concerns. Although it has been shown that "the P.Q. victory [in 1976] was greatly facilitated by the party's decision to dissociate the election from a decision on independence",[16] the separatism/independence issue has been the bedrock on which support for the Parti Québécois has been established and sustained. Moreover, although public-opinion polls demonstrate that the growth of nationalist sentiments in Quebec has been slow, the evidence of the polarizing effect of political socialization in Canada suggests that these sentiments will continue to grow apace as successive generations of new and discontented citizens reach the age of majority and enter the political process. It is, after all, the French Canadians who were adolescents in the 1960s who, today, are most committed to Quebec independence and are the strongest supporters of the Parti Québécois.

We noted in Chapter 4 that patriotism, a sense of community, and confidence in the political process are important prerequisites for most forms of citizen participation. It is reasonable to speculate, therefore, that insofar as the influence of the United States and the competition between levels of government have divided citizen loyalties and nurtured suspicions of the inferiority of Canadian institutions, political participation probably has suffered. More certain is that these developments are responsible for the relatively greater participation in provincial and local affairs observed in chapters 2 and 3.

Nevertheless, although it also is sometimes suggested that the comparative disaffection of Francophone Canadians for federal institutions increases the likelihood of political violence, there is little evidence to sustain the view.[17] This may be, in part, as Jean Pierre Richert contends, because French-Canadian youth is socialized into a "pattern of authority [that] remains authoritarian, or at least paternalistic", in spite of the effects of the many political, social, and economic changes that have occurred in Quebec during the past fifty years.[18] In part, as well, the reduction in French-Canadian political violence since the early 1970s may be due to the federal structure of Canadian government which made possible the rise of René Lévesque and the Parti Québécois thereby providing a legitimate, non-violent outlet for French-Canadian disaffection and dissent.

POLITICAL ATTITUDES

Although loyalty to the community and a positive evaluation of government facilitate participation, variations in the form and intensity of political involvement depend more directly on the nature of specific political attitudes and individual role perceptions. Prominent in the latter categories, as noted in chapters 4 and 5, are a generalized political interest, a sense of political efficacy, and a commitment to a political party or ideology.

An interest in politics can begin at any age and for a variety of reasons. Some citizens develop a rudimentary interest in limited aspects of politics as early as age three or four. Others remain apathetic into middle age. Still others never become interested in politics. For most citizens, however, an interest in politics is acquired during adolescence or the early adult years and fluctuates in intensity thereafter.[19]

When and how strongly political interest develops depends largely on the "politicization" or political content of the environment. Children reared by politically active parents or in families where political discussions are commonplace tend to develop early, intense, and enduring political commitments. So, to a lesser extent, do students whose friends and classmates are interested in politics or whose teachers incorporate political discussions into the curriculum. Of course, an especially dramatic political event or crisis can stimulate the interest of an entire generation if not the whole population, as the war in Vietnam did for the generation who came to political consciousness in the United States during the 1960s. On a smaller scale, some have suggested that the controversial personality of Prime Minister Trudeau has increased public interest in recent Canadian elections to a degree that would not have been likely had a less emotive figure carried the Liberal standard.[20] That political interest in the 1974 national election was substantially higher than the public's general interest in politics at the same time (see Chapter 4) supports this speculation.

Whatever the agents of political socialization (and we shall have more to say about this subject in a later section), an early interest in politics is a primary characteristic distinguishing participants from nonparticipants in most activities. The younger the citizen becomes interested, the greater the likelihood he will vote, participate in political campaigns, work for a political party, seek election to public office, and even rise to a position of leadership in parliament.

The fact that a concern for politics acquired in childhood influences the political behaviour of adults twenty years or more later is due to the tendency of political interest to intensify political learning. In the same way that politically interested adults are more sensitive to the political stimuli they encounter, the child who is interested in politics is more likely to perceive and be receptive to the political lessons of youth. He gains a head start in developing the political skills necessary for participation and, because learning is continuous, the advantage seized in childhood is not easy for others to make up.

Frequently called the structuring principle, the belief that childhood learning conditions the development of adult attitudes thereby *indirectly* structuring adult behaviour is one of two basic assumptions supporting political-socialization research. The other, the primacy principle, holds that political attitudes learned early in life continue to exercise a *direct* influence on the political behaviour of adults.[21] One political attitude whose effects conform to the primacy principle is party identification. Among the earliest political attitudes acquired and one of the most enduring, the influence of partisanship on adult behaviour has been extensively documented.[22]

Although partisan loyalties develop later in Canada than in the United States, most Canadians identify with a political party before they become interested in politics or are able to distinguish the leaders and policies of different parties. The average age at which these loyalties develop varies by region and province. In general, however, about a third of the public identifies with a party by Grade 4; nearly sixty per cent are committed by Grade 8; and fewer than one-quarter remains uncommitted past the age of eighteen.[23]

Like patriotism, partisan loyalties are emotionally based and comparatively resistant to change. Where both parents support the same political party and the child is aware of their choice, it is a remarkable child who is able to resist the unspoken pressure to conform. Similarly, the student who is uncommitted when he enters school confronts a variety of pressures, some less subtle than others, to seek the approval of friends by adopting the prevailing party loyalty of his group. If cross-pressures develop because there is disagreement in the group or because parental loyalties conflict, individuals frequently resolve the emotional dilemma either by proclaiming their political neutrality or by becoming apathetic.

Not quite one-third of the public change party loyalties during their lives, typically as young adults and frequently in response to countervailing pressures from friends or from new ideas encountered in college or precipitated by political crisis.[24] To a significant degree, therefore, party loyalties are "inherited". They are passed from one generation to the next, stoutly defended, and only occasionally re-evaluated. This is not to say that party loyalties are necessarily incongruent with the values of the citizen. Because political interests in Canada frequently divide along social, economic, and ethnic lines, the limited social-mobility characteristic of Canadian society insures a relatively high correlation between the goals of parents and their children. That the rationality of partisan behaviour is largely coincidental, however, can provide little comfort to contemporary democrats and the advocates of increased political participation.

Unlike partisan loyalties, many other attitudes, especially those pertaining to specific issues and policies, are acquired, altered, and abandoned with relative ease. Between these two extremes lie attitudes about personal political efficacy. Typically, its development proceeds along two distinct but related paths. On the one hand, individuals in democratic polities are continually exposed to a series of explicit lessons about the political system and their relationship to it. Students are taught in the schools that Canada is a democratic society and that citizens possess both a right and a responsibility to participate in politics, by voting in particular. At the same time, students have numerous opportunities to learn by doing and to practice the lessons of citizenship not only by participating in student government, mock elections, and classroom simulations of democratic processes but also by joining political clubs, working for political parties and in election campaigns, taking part in community-action programs, joining political protest activities, or participating in the myriad other activities where opportunities are unrestricted by age. The individual's reaction to such experiences—whether positive or negative, successful or unsuccessful—creates an impression of the political process and its susceptibility to individual influence that conditions political attitudes and behaviour for years thereafter.[25]

On the other hand, because political efficacy is closely related to broader feelings of personal competence, it is indirectly influenced by individual experiences in non-political areas as well. Children who consistently fail in the classroom, on the athletic field, or in their social relations are likely to carry a sense of inferiority into the political arena. The same is true of children reared in authoritarian families, those who attend schools where student participation is minimal, and adults whose occupations provide few opportunities for self-management.[26] Even a vicarious experience of failure resulting from a perception of the inadequacies of one's family, identity group, or nation, can contribute to feelings of personal inadequacy and political incompetence, and thus prejudice the individual against political activity.

FROM WHOM AND HOW?

Few aspects of the political socialization process have benefited from as much research as the sources of political learning. Those responsible for civic education occupy a critical position in society. They serve as guardians of the civic culture, defenders of political order, and agents of social and political change.

Numerous individuals and institutions contribute to political learning including the family, school, peer group, friends, the media, voluntary groups, public institutions, and the government. Although controversy persists regarding the relative importance of the different sources, the prevailing view has been that "the family incubates political man"[27] and is the foremost agent of political socialization. Critics of this view concede the importance of family, especially in transmitting basic orientations, but challenge its pre-eminence in other areas. Their contention is that the role of the family in the development of more specific political attitudes and behaviour is secondary, and consists largely of supporting the more important influences of school and peer group. According to Pammett this is particularly evident in Canada where political attitudes develop several years later than in the United States and where, as a consequence, most political learning occurs at an age when school and peer group enjoy maximum influence.[28] Substantial evidence can be marshalled in support of both positions. Indeed it is arguable that much of this controversy is misplaced and stems from the very different perspectives of the several authors.

What the evidence suggests is that no individual or institution is consistently more important than the others. Instead, the influence of different agents fluctuate according to the agents' relationships with the individual, the individual's psychological maturity, and the timing of what is learned.

It is conventional to distinguish agents on the basis of their political content or purposes. Political agents are defined as those whose political content is overt and who are established specifically for political purposes. Examples include political parties, civic education courses, partisan political broadcasts, and political clubs and youth groups. Although the political content of these agents is more visible and intense than that of such non-political agents as family, friends, and neighbours, the latter are generally more important sources of political education. This is because political agents are usually linked to individuals by a series of secondary relationships which tend to be highly structured, formal, and impersonal, whereas non-political agents compensate by establishing strong primary bonds of mutual affection and respect.[29] The family environment is usually among the least politicized; but because of the emotional ties of the individual to the family, the political lessons which the family does convey tend to leave an indelible impression.

Political learning depends as much on the individual's psychological maturity as on the nature of the educating agent. According to Jean Piaget,[30] the intellectual capacity of the individual develops slowly during childhood and adolescence in two principal directions. First, during these formative years, the child's perceptual horizons expand and become increasingly decentralized. From an initial preoccupation with self and parents the infant gradually becomes aware of more distant relatives and friends and, finally, of a variety of secondary agents. Simultaneously, the child matures intellectually. Limited initially to relatively primitive and largely non-rational modes of learning, the child progressively develops the capacity to learn through more sophisticated and rational processes.

Regarding the latter, Hess and Torney argue that different models of learning characterize different learning situations.[31] Where what is learned is essentially factual or cognitive, the learning process frequently conforms to an *accumulation* model. This involves the continual addition of more and more sophisticated "bits" of information and would characterize political education in school. The child who knows that Canada is governed by Parliament is subsequently taught that Parliament is composed of the Senate and the House of Commons and later still that the House of Commons is an elected body with substantially greater powers than the Senate. The learning of political roles more often fits an *interpersonal transfer* model. This assumes that individuals learn by drawing analogies between new political situations and previous non-political experiences. For example, children who perceive a similarity between their fathers' role as head of family and the role of the prime minister as leader of the country are likely to ascribe attributes they associate with their fathers, such as honesty, authority and affection, to the prime minister.

Still other political attitudes, partisan loyalties in particular, are learned through a process of imitation or *identification*. Most parents do not consciously teach their children to identify with a political party. Children pick up clues to their parents' beliefs and adopt them as their own in an attempt to secure parental approval and affection. Finally, lessons of a more subtle, complex, and abstract nature are frequently learned through a *cognitive-development* model. Individuals who have achieved a high level of intellectual maturity are able to learn independently by applying the rules of logic to personal observation and experience. Opinions regarding public-policy issues occasionally develop in this manner.

The stages of intellectual development further help to explain why timing is important—political lessons are learned differently according to when they are learned. The earlier political lessons occur the greater is the likelihood they will be influenced by primary and non-political agents and learned through non-rational processes. They also will be less susceptible to change. Party identifications, we observed, are among the first political orientations acquired. Thus they tend to be learned from the family through non-rational processes and are comparatively resistant to change. In contrast opinions about specific issues and policies—among the last political attitudes acquired—are highly volatile. They change continually in response to relatively minor fluctuations in the political environment, whereas major realignments in party loyalties occur on average once every two or three decades and are usually precipitated by dramatic political, social, or economic upheaval.

SOCIALIZING DEMOCRATIC CITIZENS

The significance of these distinctions lies in their implications for democratic theory and, in particular, for the prospects of motivating wider and more rational citizen participation in Canada. Notwithstanding that political learning can occur at any age, the fact that fundamental aspects of political personality are acquired early and resist change limits the possibilities for expanding participation by re-educating current generations of adults. Although marginal increases could be achieved by eliminating the few remaining obstacles to participation in Canada, significant increases are more likely to be achieved through changes in the initial political socialization of the young.

A problem, however, is that early political learning is dominated by primary and non-political agents. Aside from the tendency of such relationships to be largely non-rational, the dominance of primary relationships poorly prepares all but a small proportion of the young for participation in the secondary institutions which monopolize adult political life. More significantly, according to Dawson and Prewitt,

> this predominant role of primary agents means that political learning for society as a whole is unorganized, decentralized, varied, and nondeliberate. The crucial role of primary groups . . . renders it difficult for the government or any central agency to completely control or manipulate political loyalties or values. . . . Even the most highly developed and techno-logically efficient governments cannot effectively oversee the political learning that takes place in these groups.[32]

What this suggests is that systematic changes in political learning are most likely to be achieved by reducing the early political influence of primary agents in favour of a corresponding increase in the influence of secondary and political agents. Such a strategy is employed in the People's Republic of China and the Soviet Union, both of which have attempted in various ways to substitute the political influence of state-controlled youth groups and civic education courses for that of the family. Nor is this strategy new. Plato advocated a somewhat similar program for the education of the guardian class in his *Republic*.[33] It is B. F. Skinner, however, who carries these proposals to their logical conclusion. In *Walden II*, his fictional account of a psychologically constructed utopia, Skinner proposes to maximize the rationality of human behaviour by separating children from parents at an early age and making education entirely a responsibility of society.

Obviously, once one begins to manipulate the socialization process to increase political participation, it is possible for the process to be used to control other aspects of human thought and behaviour as well. And if this occurs, what has become of the human freedom and individual self-development that increased participation is intended to secure?

SUMMARY

Political attitudes and behaviour are learned. Citizen apathy, intolerance, and political inactivity as well as their opposites are products of long and complicated processes of political socialization. Although many aspects of this process remain mysterious, substantial progress has been made during the past two decades in understanding the content, process, and dynamics of political learning. Knowledge of this process creates the potential to use political socialization to change the structure of citizen participation in society. But are such changes desirable? What are the likely consequences of increased participation for the individual and society? And can the possible benefits justify the loss of individual freedom which centralization of political socialization appears to imply? The remainder of this volume addresses these concerns.

NOTES

1. John Stuart Mill, "On Liberty", in *Utilitarianism, Liberty and Representative Government* (New York, 1951), p. 186.
2. John W. Whiting and Irvin L. Child, *Child Training and Personality: A Cross-Cultural Study* (New Haven, 1963), p. 63.
3. Roberta Siegel, "Assumptions about the Learning of Political Values", *The Annals of the American Academy of Political and Social Science,* Vol. 361 (1965), p. 1. Similar definitions are advanced in: Herbert Hyman, *Political Socialization* (New York, 1959), p. 17; and Gabriel Almond, "Introduction: A Functional Approach to Comparative Politics", in G. Almond and J. S. Coleman, eds., *The Politics of Developing Areas* (Princeton, 1960), p. 27.

4. David Easton and Jack Dennis, *Children in the Political System* (New York, 1969), p. 7. See also, Kenneth Langton, *Political Socialization* (New York, 1969), pp. 4-5; and Fred I Greenstein, "Political Socialization", *International Encyclopedia of the Social Sciences* (New York, 1965), p. 551.
5. Greenstein, ibid., pp. 552-53.
6. E. D. Lawson, "Flag Preferences of Canadians: Before the Maple Leaf", *Psychological Reports,* Vol. 17 (1965), pp. 553-54.
7. Stephen H. Ullman, "The Socialization of Orientations Toward Canada: A Study of Cape Breton Whites and Indians", in Jon H. Pammett and Michael S. Whittington, eds., *Foundations of Political Culture: Political Socialization in Canada* (Toronto, 1976), pp. 280-84.
8. Jon H. Pammett and Michael S. Whittington, "Introduction: Political Culture and Political Socialization," in Pammett and Whittington, ibid., pp. 17-21.
9. Donald Higgins, "The Political Americanization of Canadian Children", in Pammett and Whittington, ibid., pp. 251-64.
10. Ullman, "The Socialization of Orientations Toward Canada", note 22, p. 287.
11. H. D. Forbes, "Conflicting National Identities Among Canadian Youth", in Pammett and Whittington, *Foundations of Political Culture,* Table 9, p. 305.
12. Ibid., Tables 2 and 10, pp. 295, 301.
13. J. C. Johnstone, *Young Peoples' Images of Canadian Society: An Opinion Survey of Canadian Youth, Thirteen to Twenty Years of Age* (Ottawa, 1967); and Paul G. Lamy, "Political Socialization of French- and English-Canadian Youth: Socialization into Discord", in Elia Zureik and Robert M. Pike, eds., *Socialization and Values in Canadian Society* (Toronto, 1975), Vol. I, pp. 263-80.
14. Johnstone, ibid., p. xvi.
15. Lamy, ibid., p. 278.
16. Maurice Pinard and Richard Hamilton, "The Parti Québécois Comes to Power: An Analysis of the 1976 Quebec Election", unpublished paper presented at a joint session of the Canadian Political Science Association and la Société Canadienne de Science Politique, Learned Societies Meetings, June 1977, p. 48. See also Richard Hamilton and Maurice Pinard, "The Bases of Parti Québécois Support in Recent Quebec Elections", *Canadian Journal of Political Science*, Vol. 9 (March 1976), pp. 3-26; and Maurice Pinard and Richard Hamilton, "The Independence Issue and the Polarization of the Electorate: The 1973 Quebec Election", *Canadian Journal of Political Science,* Vol. 10 (June 1977), pp. 215-60.
17. Wayne G. Reilly, "Political Attitudes Among Law Students in Quebec", *Canadian Journal of Political Science,* Vol. 4 (March 1971), esp. Table VII.

18. "Political Socialization in Quebec", *Canadian Journal of Political Science,* Vol. 6 (June 1973), p. 312.
19. Allan Kornberg, Joel Smith, and David Bromley, "Some Differences in the Political Socialization Patterns of Canadian and American Party Officials: A Preliminary Report", *Canadian Journal of Political Science,* Vol. 2 (March 1969), pp. 64-68; and William Mishler "Political Participation and the Process of Political Socialization in Canada", Ph.D. Thesis, Duke University, 1972, chapters 4-6.
20. See, for example, G. R. Winham and R. B. Cunningham, "Party Leader Images in the 1968 Federal Election", *Canadian Journal of Political Science,* Vol. 3 (March 1970).
21. Recently, the validity of both the structuring principle and the primacy principle have been challenged, albeit on the basis of research flawed in fundamental respects. The original criticism is presented in Donald D. Searing, Joel J. Schwartz, and Alden E. Lind, "The Structuring Principle: Political Socialization and Belief Systems", *American Political Science Review,* Vol. 67 (June 1973), pp. 415-32; and Donald D. Searing, Gerald Wright, and George Rabinowitz, "The Primacy Principle: Attitude Change and Political Socialization", *British Journal of Political Science* (January 1976), pp. 83-114. For a lively discussion of the methodology of the former see the "Communications" by Fred I. Greenstein and James Clarke and Henry Kenski and the rejoinder by Searing, *et al.* in the *American Political Science Review*, Vol. 68 (June 1974), pp. 720-29.
22. The most recent discussion of the nature and effects of partisanship in Canada is Harold D. Clarke, *et al., Political Choice in Canada* (Toronto, 1979), chapters 5 and 10.
23. Jon H. Pammett, "The Development of Political Orientations in Canadian School Children", *Canadian Journal of Political Science,* Vol. 4 (March 1971), pp. 137-39; Pammett and Whittington, "Introduction", Figure 7, p. 25; and Alan Gregg and Michael Whittington, "Regional Variations in Children's Political Attitudes", in D. J. Bellamy, J. H. Pammett, and D. C. Rowat, *The Provincial Political Systems* (Toronto, 1976), pp. 77-80.
24. Clarke, *et al., Political Choices in Canada,* Chapter 5 and William Mishler, *et al.,* "Patterns of Political Socialization: Simulating the Development of Party Identification in Two Political Elites", *Comparative Political Studies,* Vol. 7 (January 1974), pp. 399-430.
25. On the nature of political socialization in Canadian schools, see A. B. Hodgetts, *What Culture? What Heritage?* (Toronto, 1968); and David Pratt, "The Social Role of School Textbooks in Canada", in Zureik and Pike, eds., *Socialization and Values in Canadian Society,* pp. 100-26; see also, Pammett's description of the political impact of an election campaign on student volunteers in "Adolescent Political Activity as a Learning Experience: The Action-

Trudeau Campaign of 1968'', in Pammett and Whittington, *Foundations of Political Culture,* pp. 160-94.
26. Evidence to this effect is reported in Gabriel A. Almond and Sidney Verba, *The Civic Culture* (Princeton, 1963), Chapter 11. On Canada, in particular, see George Watson and Allan Kornberg, "The Family and School as Agents in Early Political Socialization", *Manitoba Journal of Education Research* (June 1968), pp. 64-73; and Mishler, "Political Participation and the Process of Political Socialization in Canada", chapters 4 and 5.
27. Robert Lane, *Political Life* (New York, 1959), p. 204.
28. See, in particular, Robert D. Hess and Judith V. Torney; *The Development of Political Attitudes in Children* (Chicago, 1968), Chapter 5; and Pammett, "Development of Political Orientations", p. 139.
29. For elaboration of these distinctions see Richard E. Dawson and Kenneth Prewitt, *Political Socialization* (Boston, 1969), pp. 99-103.
30. Jean Piaget, *The Psychology of Intelligence* (London, 1947); and *The Moral Judgment of the Child* (New York, 1965).
31. Hess and Torney, *The Development of Political Attitudes in Children,* Chapter I.
32. Dawson and Prewitt, *Political Socialization,* p. 101.
33. Although Plato did not propose separating parents from their children he did advocate that the state "induce mothers and nurses to tell their children only those [stories] which we have approved, and to think more of moulding their souls with these stories than they now do of rubbing their limbs . . .", *The Republic of Plato,* trans. by F. M. Cornford (New York, 1968), p. 69.

7.

The Consequences
of Participation

Among the more important issues in democratic theory, and one of the most neglected, is the question of the consequences of participation for citizens and society. In Chapter 1, we noted that classical democratic theorists advocated extensive citizen involvement in the affairs of government not only as a means of identifying the majority's will and reaching collective decisions, but also as a stimulus to individual education and moral development. Elitist democratic theories, in contrast, rest on the view that limited participation is necessary to insure government accountability and responsiveness but caution that excessive participation can jeopardize political stability and undermine the liberal substance of democracy.

Three specific issues underlie this disagreement: whether and to what extent the nature and level of citizen participation influence the selection of political leaders and the formulation of public policy; whether increased participation would raise the level of political conflict and instability; and whether and to what extent political activity conditions citizen attitudes and individual moral development. This chapter considers each of these concerns.

PARTICIPATION, LEADERSHIP, AND PUBLIC POLICY

The belief that political leaders and public policies ought to be responsive to the expressed interests of the body politic distinguishes democratic theories and is a fundamental tenet of most of the various formulations of the classical democratic and democratic elitist approaches. Consistent with their utilitarian heritage, classical theories typically assume that citizens are the best judges of their own interests—that they are best qualified to determine "whether their shoes pinch and where"—and that political activity is the most effective and efficient means to express individual interests and render judgment on the representatives' response.[1] As a practical matter, the classical democrats acknowledge that citizen participation may have to be limited to the selection of political leaders, but they strongly defend the need for equivalent levels of participation among all social and economic strata believing that the interests of less active groups suffer relative neglect. According to John Stuart Mill:

> We need not suppose that when power resides in an exclusive class, that class will knowingly and deliberately sacrifice the other classes to themselves: it suffices that, in the absence of its natural defenders, the interest of the excluded is always in danger of being overlooked; and, when looked at, is seen with very different eyes from those of the person whom it directly concerns.[2]

Although less certain that citizens know their real interests,[3] the elitists concede that some degree of participation is necessary for political accountability and responsiveness. They are more willing than the classical theorists, however, to limit participation to electoral forms (primarily voting) and to tolerate relatively large variations in the political involvement of different social groups. Elitist theories hold, instead, that political leaders are generally better equipped by virtue of their more extensive educations and greater political experience, to assess the public interest and decide matters of public policy than is the comparatively uninformed, apathetic, and less tolerant electorate. Therefore, elitist theories conclude, political leaders ought to be left relatively unencumbered by the demands of more extensive citizen participation.[4]

Although it is apparent in chapters 3 and 5 that citizen participation in Canada assumes largely electoral forms and differs substantially among social and economic groups, the evidence regarding the leadership and policy consequences of these patterns is ambiguous. It is arguable, for example, that the disproportionate number of social and economic elites in parliament and the provincial assemblies at least partly reflects the higher level of political activity characteristic of the upper socio-economic strata of Canadian society.[5] This view is supported by the fact that the proportion of public notables in parliament has declined with the expansion of the electorate and the democratization of the voting lists. Thus, according to Kornberg,

> . . . 43 per cent of the freshmen members [of parliament] were notables during the period from 1867 to 1896 when the electorate was small and property-based. As the proportions of the population eligible for enfranchisement rose (1900-1917) the percentage of freshmen notables elected declined to 21 per cent, and has dropped to 11 per cent since universal suffrage was achieved in 1921.[6]

On the other hand, the establishment of women's suffrage in 1921 and the steady growth in the proportion of women voters in the ensuing twenty years did not produce appreciable gains in the numbers of women elected to public office. Even now women comprise less than five per cent of parliament and the various provincial assemblies. Nor does it appear that lowering the federal voting age from twenty-one to eighteen has appreciably reduced the historic under-representation of the young. Citizens between eighteen and forty years of age continue to be the most under-represented age group in parliament.[7]

Although the composition of the political leadership has never mirrored Canadian society and has responded slowly and unevenly to changes in the electorate, it remains to be determined whether under-represented interests have been neglected. Little evidence is available regarding the relationship between leadership composition and policy responsiveness in Canada, but what there is provides only limited support for either the classical democratic or democratic elitist positions. A recent study of parliamentary and social change in Canada reports a strong connection between the composition of the House of Commons and the type of legislation enacted during the first twenty-seven parliaments. Although much of this relationship can be attributed to antecedent environmental factors such as the structure of society and the vitality of the economy, the authors report several important instances where substantial changes in public policy have resulted directly from changes in the membership of parliament. In particular, they conclude that parliament has been most responsive to the needs of disadvantaged groups when the governing party has failed to control an over-all majority of seats in parliament and when minor parties have achieved substantial representation.[8]

Similarly, at the provincial level, it has been observed that the composition of the legislative assemblies has been the strongest determinant of government responsiveness to public health-care needs over the past half-century. Although economic considerations also are important, the most responsive provinces consistently have been those in which minor parties—the CCF/NDP, in particular—have enjoyed their greatest successes.[9]

What these studies suggest is that the composition of Canada's political leadership has contributed to the changing content of public policy and the responsiveness of policies to public interest. Consistent with the classical theories of democracy these studies clearly indicate that where changes in the composition of the political leadership have occurred, public policy has responded. Indeed, even relatively modest increases in the representation of disadvantaged groups have resulted in substantial benefits. None the less, the composition of the leadership does not appear to be the sole or even the primary determinant of policy responsiveness. Public policies frequently have reflected societal trends in the absence of significant leadership change suggesting, as elitist theories contend that in some cases, the threat of leadership change posed by the existence of relatively competitive political parties and periodic elections may be sufficient to insure minimum levels of accountability.

There is less reason to believe that the aggregate level of citizen participation influences policies more directly. Several studies have explored the relationship between voter turnout and various types of public policy at both the federal and provincial levels. Although turnout appears to have some effect on distributive policies, such as the level of social-welfare expenditure, these relationships have been consistently small, usually spurious, and frequently contrary to the predicted direction (i.e., higher levels of turnout are linked with lower government welfare expenditures).[10]

But if the general level of voter turnout has little bearing on the nature of public policy, the voting levels of specific groups can be critical. Since a government's resources invariably are insufficient to meet the needs and demands of every group, it seems reasonable, as classical theory predicts, that the allocation of resources will favour the most active:

> During a snowstorm the plows have to begin on one street rather than another. Is it not more rational for officials to start in the section with more votes cast per street?. . . If garbage funds are limited and sacrifices must be made, should a rational politician cut services equally or should he decide to retain backdoor collection . . . in the high turnout areas while requiring residents of poorer [and thus lower turnout] areas to place the garbage cans on the street for curb collection?[11]

Hough's study of voter turnout in Toronto vindicates his belief that rational politicians are more responsive to the interests of more active groups. Higher turnout areas in Toronto do receive better snow removal, garbage collection, and other social services than areas with lower voting participation levels.[12] Although comparable studies have not been undertaken at the federal level in Canada research in the United States suggests the phenomenon is a general one. Specifically it has been reported that participants and non-participants differ both in their perceptions of the important political issues and their preferences among alternative solutions. And where these differences exist, political leaders are considerably more likely to share the preferences of the more active strata.[13]

Comparisons of the extent of citizen participation in several political activities other than voting with levels of provincial responsiveness on three indicators of social-welfare policy suggest that increased participation is associated with lower levels of responsiveness (Table 7:1). Citizens in the Atlantic provinces, for example, are among the most economically disadvantaged but most politically active in the nation. Nevertheless, their provincial governments rank at or near the bottom in social-welfare

Table 7:1 RANKINGS OF TEN PROVINCES ON FIVE MEASURES OF CITIZEN PARTICIPATION AND THREE MEASURES OF PROVINCIAL SOCIAL WELFARE EXPENDITURES, 1974

Province	Voting	Campaigning	Communicating	Community Activity	Total Activity	Total Soc. Welfare Expenditures	Soc. Welfare Expenditures Per Capita	Soc. Welfare Expenditures As a % of Total Expend.
Nfld.	9.5	1	7.5	6	6	9	9	10
P.E.I.	1	2	4	2	1	10	4	8
N.S.	5.5	3	5	3	3	8	10	9
N.B.	2.5	4	9.5	4	4	7	5	7
Que.	8	5.5	7.5	9.5	9	1	1.5	2
Ont.	4	7	3	7	5	2	8	6
Man.	7	9	9.5	9.5	10	5	6	4
Sask.	2.5	8	2	1	2	6	7	5
Alta.	9.5	5.5	6	5	8	4	3	3
B.C.	5.5	10	1	8	7	3	1.5	1

SOURCES: Provincial Rankings on Citizen Participation are based on data from the 1974 National Election Study. Expenditure rankings are based on data published by Statistics Canada, *Provincial Government Finance.*

expenditures, welfare expenditures per capita, and the percentage of all expenditures devoted to welfare. In contrast, Alberta, British Columbia, and Quebec lead the way in welfare expenditures in spite of the fact that their citizens, on average, are the most affluent and least politically active in Canada.

This does not mean, however, that higher levels of participation necessarily reduce government responsiveness. An alternative explanation is simply that the Atlantic provinces cannot afford to spend as much on welfare as more affluent provinces. Indeed, given the differences previously observed in the backgrounds and political attitudes of participants and non-participants in all activities (but especially the more demanding ones), it is reasonable to speculate that the upper-class bias of higher-level activities contributes to the negative relationship between participation and responsiveness. Presumably, therefore, were participation by the members of disadvantaged groups to increase and sufficient resources provided their provincial governments, the interests of the disadvantaged would more likely be reflected in public policy.

Of course, all of the activities reported in Table 7:1 involve the direct participation of individual citizens in the selection of public officials or in attempts to influence government decisions. According to elitist theories, however, direct political action not only exceeds the capabilities of many citizens but also is unnecessary for insuring government accountability. The elitists' argument, briefly recapitulated, is that political parties and interest groups provide significant indirect channels of participation and influence by serving as political middlemen, or "linkage mechanisms", between citizens and government. By aggregating and organizing individuals with common interests and beliefs and, then, articulating these groups' interests in the electoral and policy processes, political parties and interest groups make fewer demands on the citizen's time and energy and enable him to speak with a louder voice than would be possible through individual activity. Porter summarizes the theory succinctly:

The public welfare is served when individuals join groups according to their interests, and, through these groups, bring pressure on institutional power-holders. Thus democracy is guaranteed when groups are strong enough to make themselves heard, when they can avail themselves of the various media of propaganda, and when they prepare briefs and act as lobbyists and pressure groups.[14]

That political parties and interest groups "are strong enough to make themselves heard" and play important roles in the development of public policy is well established. What is uncertain, however, is whether either type of organization provides sufficient links between citizen and government to substitute for direct citizen participation in politics. What most elitist theories overlook is that the structure of power within these organizations is highly oligarchic and provides few opportunities for effective rank-and-file participation in organization affairs.

Political parties, for example, play an important role in shaping public policy, but only a small minority of citizens become involved in party activities or have the opportunity to participate in the formulation of party principals and the selection of party candidates for public office. Even those who become involved and participate in party leadership conventions frequently have little effective voice in determining party policy. As observed in Chapter 3, despite the adoption of reforms by both major parties designed to increase member participation in party affairs, the most important decisions within the party continue to be made at the top where power is concentrated in the hands of a small group of party elites, many of whom are, themselves, elected public officials. Moreover, party leaders are not, in any sense, representative of party identifiers in the electorate. To the contrary, party activists are social and economic as well as political elites and differ significantly from party identifiers in the electorate on a number of fundamental issues.[15]

Interest groups in Canada also are accorded substantial weight in the formulation of public policy. The problem, again, however, is that interest groups are poorly representative of the public interest. For one thing, nearly forty per cent of adult Canadians are not members of any interest group and only about one-fourth or one-third of these groups are politically relevant.[16] For another, those who are members frequently are not aware of the political activities of group leaders and have few effective opportunities to influence the political positions which the leaders take in the name of their membership. According to Porter, "In Canada, as in similar countries, most associations have a membership too dispersed to exercise effective control over leaders and permanent officials. . . . [L]eaders can be thrown out and permanent officials fired, but they rarely are, . . . because the membership has come to depend on their expertise and knowledge."[17] The problem is exacerbated because, as in political parties, interest-group elites are often unrepresentative of the rank and file, differing substantially both in background and opinion.

Although public policy is responsive to interest-group demands and party programs, there is more than a suspicion that interest-group demands and party programs are produced as a result of the activities of a small and unrepresentative group of political, social, and economic elites. According to Robert Presthus,

> In the context of democratic participation, the going system also produces some questionable consequences. Participation tends to be restricted to those groups that possess the greatest amounts of political resources. . . . The majority are unable to compete effectively in the political arena, for lack of such resources . . . [which] tend to be monopolized by those we have defined as political elites. Government in responding mainly to [the elites], is placed in the somewhat anomalous position of defending the strong against the weak.[18]

Interest groups and political parties are not agents of the common man nor are they substitutes for widespread citizen activity. To the contrary, increasing citizen participation in interest-group and party activities seems likely to increase the responsiveness of these organizations to member interests, particularly to the interests of the disadvantaged. In political parties and interest groups, as in other areas of political life, Mill's caution appears well founded—"in the absence of its natural defenders, the interest of the excluded is always in danger of being overlooked."

Finally, with regard to the policy consequences of political protest, the meager evidence available provides little comfort to those who view protest as a effective means to challenge government priorities and alter the direction of public policy. Indeed we have noted that the typical response to political protest in Canada has been swift and often harsh retaliation. Even comparatively well-organized, affluent, and upper-status groups have achieved little through political protest. To cite but one example, although the doctors' strike in Saskatchewan following the adoption of a provincial health-insurance program in 1962 led to the demotion of the responsible minister and probably contributed to the defeat of the CCF government in 1964, the doctors failed to achieve their specific goal of repealing the offending legislation, and, according to one account, severely weakened the internal unity and political standing of the doctors' association in the attempt.[19]

The relationship between citizen participation, political leadership, and public policy in Canada is not a simple one. A paucity of systematic research combined with conflicting evidence have confused as much as clarified the matter. Nevertheless, several tentative conclusions are suggested. Among the most certain is that the nature of political participation does affect political life. Although aggregate levels of activity have little impact on the composition of the leadership or the content of policy, unequal rates of participation among social segments appear to contribute to the upper-class bias of both.

On balance, there is substantial support for the democratic elitist contention that widespread and intense citizen participation is not necessary for political accountability or responsiveness; minimal levels of participation will suffice. However, an equally persuasive case exists for the classical democratic view that there must be equivalent levels of participation among groups if equitable representation of all political interests is to obtain. The political leadership in Canada does not appear to have "knowingly and deliberately sacrificed the other classes to themselves"; but it does seem to have accorded somewhat greater consideration to the interests of the more active members of society.

POLITICAL PARTICIPATION AND EDUCATION

As has been noted, the classical democratic emphasis on citizen participation rests not only on the instrumental value of participation for political accountability and responsiveness but also on its educational value for intellectual growth and moral development. If this argument is correct then increased participation would be warranted even if it does not contribute to political accountability or responsiveness. Unfortunately, even less is known about the individual consequences of political activity than about its consequences for public policy. Research on this relationship is in its infancy and little of that which has been conducted has focused specifically on Canada. Therefore, in attempting to assess this critical issue in the democratic debate it is necessary to rely on observations derived from studies in other western societies and to adjust these observations, insofar as possible, to the Canadian context.

As has been noted at several points, there is ample evidence documenting the association between higher levels of citizen participation and a variety of civic virtues both in Canada and elsewhere.[20] Those who participate more often in all of the many varieties of political endeavour are generally better informed about politics and current political issues; they are more likely to be interested in politics and public affairs and to feel capable of influencing the direction of political life; and they demonstrate, on average, greater tolerance of dissent and concern for the political rights of minorities. Moreover, the association between participation and the democratic virtues increases with the intensity of political activity. Thus citizens who participate in political campaigns, work for political parties or community action groups, seek public office, or communicate with public officials are more likely to possess these traits and to a greater degree than citizens who either do not participate in political life or confine their involvement to lower-level activities, such as voting.

It is true, of course, that correlations between different political activities and various attributes of democratic citizenship permit several interpretations. In particular, the available evidence is insufficient to determine whether increased participation enhances political information, efficacy, and tolerance or vice versa. The most likely possibility, however, is that their influence is reciprocal; political interest, information, and efficacy and a commitment to democratic norms promote individual political involvement which reinforces, in turn, the attributes of good citizenship.

That political participation contributes to civic education is further suggested by an extensive body of literature on the effects of individual participation in non-political institutions including, in particular, the family, school, voluntary groups, and the workplace. There is increasing evidence from Canada and elsewhere that the structure of political authority within which children and adolescents are reared and educated leaves indelible marks on their later-life political personalities and behaviour.[21] Children reared in homes in which decisions are shared by the parents and in which the children's opinions are solicited and respected are more likely to develop confidence in their own opinions and a willingness to listen to and respect the opinions of others. They are also more likely to develop a healthy respect for authority. On the other hand, students educated in highly structured, authoritarian environments in which teachers predominantly lecture and student discussion is rarely permitted not only are less likely to absorb and respond to their lessons but also are more likely also to develop a sense of inferiority and powerlessness, to become less tolerant of and hostile towards others, and to develop more authoritarian personality traits.[22]

Not only children but adults as well are susceptible to the democratizing influence of participation in non-political institutions. As early as 1943, Joseph Schumpeter, one of the earliest of the modern critics of the classical theory, observed that individuals who were active in voluntary associations were both more likely to participate in politics and less likely to hold authoritarian attitudes than either citizens who were not members of voluntary groups or who, if members, were not active. Even among manual workers, whose disproportionately authoritarian personalities convinced Kornhauser of the need to limit mass participation, those active in voluntary groups were only half as likely to exhibit anti-democratic attitudes as other workers.[23]

It is the workplace, however, which is the focus of adult life and whose authority structure, according to Almond and Verba, "is probably the most significant—and salient—structure of that kind with which the average man finds himself in daily contact."[24] Consistent with the views of philosophers as diverse as John Stuart Mill, Karl Marx, Eric Fromm, and C. Wright Mills, research over the past quarter-century has produced overwhelming evidence demonstrating that worker participation in industrial decisions produces substantial benefits not only for the individual but for industry and society.[25] The availability of opportunities for effective participation in decisions affecting one's work enhances worker satisfaction, increases productivity and the quality of work produced, and reduces individual alienation, aggression, and hostility. Regarding the first of these effects, Paul Blumberg concludes:

> There is hardly a study in the literature which fails to demonstrate that satisfaction in work is enhanced or that other generally acknowledged beneficial consequences accrue from a genuine increase in workers' decision-making power . . . . [I]t is almost a matter of common sense that men will take greater pleasure and pride in their work if they are allowed to participate in shaping the policies and decisions which affect that work.[26]

More generally, participation in a democratic work environment fosters democratic personalities. Tannenbaum reports, for example, that basic personality traits can be affected by changes in the structure of industrial authority, the tendency being for personality to move in the direction of congruence with the environment.[27] Thus citizens exposed to participatory environments tend to develop more democratic personalities, whereas those subjected to autocratic environments develop authoritarian traits. Blumberg concludes from his review of this literature that industrial democracy and the opportunities it provides for individual participation and self-control "creates appropriate values, attitudes, and expectations. In other words, the organization that permits participation ultimately produces individuals who are responsible to participation."[28]

On the basis of this evidence, it is apparent that the educative argument has substantial merit. Citizens do learn by participation. Participation in basic social institutions contributes to participation in political life even as involvement at one level of the political process or in one type of political activity encourages other forms and levels of activity. Moreover, participation in whatever form is conducive to democracy; it strengthens individual self-esteem, broadens and deepens political understanding, and fosters tolerance and respect for political authority. Far from providing a justification for restricted participation, the relationship between participation and the democratic virtues provides compelling evidence of both the need to expand the structure of participation in Canada and the feasibility of such an undertaking.

PARTICIPATION AND POLITICAL STABILITY

A final criticism of increased participation is that it would undermine political stability and contribute to the erosion of authority. The arguments supporting this view are familiar and have been raised at several points. To recapitulate; first, those citizens who are least active in political life are said also to be among the least sympathetic to democratic norms. They are held, therefore, to be most susceptible to authoritarian appeals. Second, it is argued that increased participation would politicize existing non-political divisions in society, polarizing public opinion and jeopardizing public consensus on fundamental values. Finally, it has been suggested that increased participation would further erode the already weak congruence which exists between patterns of political and non-political authority in society thereby threatening the "persistence, . . . decisional efficacy, and authenticity" of democratic government.[29]

Despite the prevalence of these and related themes throughout the literature, the evidence adduced in their support is remarkably weak, largely circumstantial, and subject to alternative and frequently contradictory interpretations. For example, although the premise regarding the weak commitment of non-participants to democratic values is probably valid,[30] the conclusion drawn from this premise, that increased participation would mobilize citizens with authoritarian attitudes and jeopardize the liberal basis for democracy, is highly suspect. Given the evidence previously cited demonstrating that authoritarian attitudes are at least partly a consequence of restricted opportunities for participation in various aspects of society, it is at least equally probable that increased participation would enhance the democratic character of less-active citizens.

Even were this not the case, there is little or no evidence linking citizen participation and political instability, especially in nations with established democratic traditions and relatively high levels of economic affluence and industrial development. Although it is obvious that extreme levels of political protest would jeopardize stability, variations in other types of political activity appear to bear little relationship to levels of political conflict and instability. Participation in most areas of Canadian political life equals or exceeds that of the United States, yet Canada ranks considerably higher than the U.S. on most indicators of political order. Similarly, although France and Italy are characterized by high levels of both instability and political participation, Britain and Sweden maintain equivalent levels of citizen participation but continue to rank among the most stable and orderly of the Anglo-European democracies. Nor are these exceptional cases. In a sophisticated study of political disorder using data from more than one hundred nations, Hibbs found that levels of political participation had virtually no effect on the level of political violence.[31] Even the frequently cited collapse of the Weimar Republic and the rise of Hitler following a sudden increase in mass participation in Germany in the early 1930s fails under scrutiny to demonstrate the danger of increasing citizen participation. Kavanagh points out that, "the increase in Germany electoral turnout between 1928 and 1932 was a mere 8 per cent, from 75 to 83 per cent, and is a poor explicator of the rise of the Nazi vote from 2 per cent to 37 per cent."[32] Increases in voter participation of a similar magnitude have occurred at the federal level in Canada on at least four occasions (1896-1900; 1911-17; 1921-30; and 1953-58) without precipitating disintegration in political order or stability.

There is even less evidence supporting the pluralist contention that increased participation would "give rise to enhanced aspirations and expectations which, if unsatisfied, galvanize individuals and groups into politics [and] in the absence of strong and adaptable political institutions . . . mean instability and violence."[33] Aside from the fact that Canadian political institutions have proven themselves remarkably strong and adaptable in the face of often severe and continuing regional, linguistic, and religious cleavages, Hibbs finds no support for Huntington's theory and concludes that the strength of political institutions is far more important than the level of social mobilization in determining a society's potential for political violence.[34] Rather than politicizing social relations, increased opportunities for participation may have the opposite effect. Such at least is the implication of the studies of industrial democracy and of Almond and Verba's research on the political cultures of Britain, Italy, Mexico, Germany, and the United States.[35]

Finally, however, if there is little basis for assuming increased authoritarianism and social polarization coincide with increased participation, there is ample evidence supporting Eckstein's proposition that democratic stability can be sustained only if patterns of political authority are congruent with the authority structures characteristic of such non-political institutions as the family, school, and workplace. That opportunities for participation in basic social institutions are closely related to political participation is clearly documented in the literature previously cited. Nevertheless, the validity of the congruence argument is insufficient to justify restrictions on political activity. Acceptance of this conclusion rests as well on Eckstein's further contention that the most important social institutions can never permit substantial participation without disastrous results. According to Eckstein:

An infant cannot be cared for democratically, or a child brought up and schooled democratically. . . . Families and schools can . . . carry on a certain amount of democratic pretense . . . but by and large they cannot carry such simula-

tion and imitation of democracy to very great lengths, if they
are not to produce warped and ineffectual human beings. . . .
The same point applies, almost as obviously, to certain relations among adults. We have every reason to think that
economic organization cannot be organized in a truly
democratic manner, at any rate not without consequences that
no one wants. . . .[36]

Although the nature of childhood socialization may be such as
to advise against democratization of the family and the schools
(though this is highly debatable and in no way substantiated by
Eckstein), it is certainly not the case that economic organizations
can never be organized democratically without undesirable consequences. On the contrary, experiments with industrial
democracy provide overwhelming evidence that worker participation in industry not only is feasible but is likely to produce
highly desirable consequences for both the individual and the
firm. That individuals generalize their orientations toward
authority from the workplace to the political arena suggests as
well that increasing industrial democracy would be healthy for
democracy. Thus rather than restricting citizen political participation because existing societal authority patterns are incongruent with democracy, a stronger argument can be made for
increasing participation in non-political institutions as a means
of elevating both the quality of life and the quality and quantity
of citizen participation in politics.

SUMMARY

This chapter has examined some of the consequences variously
ascribed to citizen participation in democratic theory in order to
assess the desirability of expanding political participation in
Canada. Consistent with elitist theories of democracy, it appears
that current levels of participation in Canada, though limited,
are sufficient to insure a moderate degree of leadership accountability and responsiveness on fundamental issues. Even fairly
substantial increases in the *aggregate* scope and intensity of
citizen activity are unlikely to produce significant changes in
either the composition and responsiveness of Canada's political

leadership or the form and substance of Candian public policy. Nevertheless, because leaders and policies do reflect the pattern of participation in society, the *composition* of the politically active strata is critical. Groups whose members are less active politically are less likely to have their interests fairly represented in the political process. Consequently, an increase specifically in the participation of less-advantaged citizens, who currently are among the least active in Canada, would go far towards redressing the relative neglect of their interests and insure a more equitable structure of political representation in the future.

Political participation also serves important educational functions. Citizen participation, whether in politics or in various non-political social and economic institutions, enhances individual self-esteem and fosters a variety of democratic attitudes and personality traits. And by strengthening the democratic character of the polity, increased participation is healthy for society as well. Increased participation reduces the level of domestic violence, increases political stability, and provides the necessary basis for establishing authentic democratic structures in society.

This is not to say, of course, that all types of political activity are equally valuable or should be expanded without limit. There are obvious practical reasons for restricting direct participation in the policy process,[37] for example, and for believing that continuously high levels of political protest would be dysfunctional in the extreme. Notwithstanding such exceptions, however, the research reported in this chapter provides convincing evidence of the desirability of expanding middle-level political activities in Canada and of increasing citizen involvement in non-political areas as well.

NOTES

1. For an excellent discussion of the decision-making functions ascribed to political participation in classical democratic theory see Dennis F. Thompson, *John Stuart Mill and Representative Government* (Princeton, 1976), esp. pp. 14-21.
2. John Staurt Mill, "Considerations on Representative Government", Book III, p. 280.

3. Walter Lippmann, in particular, distrusted public opinion in these matters. See, for example, his discussion of such weaknesses in *Public Opinion* (New York, 1922), pp. 3-158.
4. Variants of this frequently repeated argument can be found in Joseph Schumpeter, *Capitalism, Socialism and Democracy* (London, 1943); Bernard Berelson, *et al., Voting* (Chicago, 1954), Chapter 14; Gabriel Almond and Sidney Verba, *The Civic Culture* (Princeton, 1963), Chapter 13; Robert Dahl, *Preface to Democratic Theory* (Chicago, 1956); and Lester W. Milbrath, *Political Participation* (Chicago, 1965), Chapter 6. A similar argument with respect to Canada has been made by Richard Van Loon, "Political Participation in Canada: The 1965 Election", *Canadian Journal of Political Science,* Vol. 3 (September 1970), pp. 376-94.
5. Evidence of the composition of parliament and the ten provincial assemblies can be found in Allan Kornberg, *et al., Legislatures and Societal Change: The Case of Canada,* Sage Research Papers in the Social Sciences, Vol. 1, Series 90-002 (Comparative Legislative Studies Series) Beverly Hills and London; Allan Kornberg and William Mishler, *Influence in Parliament: Canada* (Durham, N.C., 1976), chapters 1 and 2; and Harold D. Clarke, *et al.,* "Backbenchers", in David J. Bellamy, *et al., The Provincial Political Systems* (Toronto, 1976), pp. 214-36.
6. Allan Kornberg, "Parliament in Canadian Society", in Allan Kornberg and Lloyd D. Musolf, *Legislatures in Developmental Perspective* (Durham, N.C., 1970), p. 85.
7. Clarke, *et al.,* "Backbenchers", p. 217.
8. Kornberg, *et al., Legislatures and Social Change*, pp. 38-49.
9. William Mishler and David Campbell, "The Healthy State: Legislative Responsiveness to Public Health Care Needs in Canada", *Comparative Politics*, Vol. 10 (July 1978), pp. 479-98. See also David J. Falcone and William Mishler, "Legislative Determinants of Provincial Health Policy in Canada", *Journal of Politics*, Vol. 39 (May 1977), pp. 345-67.
10. David J. Falcone, "Legislative Change and Policy Change: A Time-Series Analysis of the Canadian House of Commons", Ph.D. Thesis, Duke University, 1975, pp. 234-44; Dale Poole, "Canadian Provincial and American State Policy", paper presented at the Annual Meeting of the Canadian Political Science Association, Montreal, June 1972; J. B. Hogan, "Social Structure and Public Policy", *Comparative Politics*, Vol. 4 (July 1972), pp. 477-509; and William Chandler, "Party Systems and Public Policy in the Canadian Provinces", paper presented at the 46th Annual Convention of the Southern Political Science Association, New Orleans, November 1974.
11. Jerry F. Hough, "Voters' Turnout and the Responsiveness of Local Governments: The Case of Toronto, 1969", in Paul Fox, ed., *Politics Canada,* 3rd ed. (Toronto, 1970), p. 294.

12. Confirmation of this relationship is provided by James Lorimer, *The Real World of City Politics* (Toronto, 1970).
13. Sidney Verba and Norman H. Nie, *Participation in America: Political Democracy and Social Equality* (New York, 1972), pp. 265-343.
14. John Porter, *The Vertical Mosaic* (Toronto, 1965), p. 556. For an elaboration of this theory with respect to political interest groups in Canada, see, Robert Presthus, *Elite Accommodation in Canadian Politics* (Toronto, 1973), pp. 3-19, 347-53. On the linkage function of political parties, see Frederick C. Englemann and Mildred A. Schwartz, *Canadian Political Parties: Origin, Character, Impact* (Scarborough, 1975), pp. 13-17; and Allan Kornberg, William Mishler, and Joel Smith, "Political Elite and Mass Perceptions of Party Locations in Issue Space: Some Tests of Two Positions", revised version printed in Kay Lawson, ed., *Political Parties and Linkage* (New Haven, 1979, forthcoming).
15. Kornberg, Mishler, and Smith, ibid., *passim*.
16. Robert Presthus, *Elites in the Policy Process* (London, 1974), p. 461.
17. Porter, *The Vertical Mosaic,* pp. 556-57.
18. Presthus, *Elites in the Policy Process,* p. 466.
19. Robin F. Badgley and Samuel Wolfe, "Medical Care and Conflict in Saskatchewan", *Milbank Memorial Fund Quarterly,* Vol. 43 (1965), pp. 463-79.
20. Evidence on these matters is reported in chapters 4-6.
21. See, for example, George Watson and Allan Kornberg, "The Family and School as Agents in Early Political Socialization", *Manitoba Journal of Educational Research* (June 1968), pp. 64-73; William Mishler, "Political Participation and the Process of Political Socialization in Canada", Ph.D. Thesis, Duke University, 1973, chapters 4-6; and Harold D. Clarke, Allan Kornberg, and James Lee, "Ontario Student Activists: A Note on Differential Participation in a Voluntary Organization", *Canadian Review of Sociology and Anthropology,* Vol. 12 (May 1975), pp. 213-20; Almond and Verba, *The Civic Culture,* Chapter 11; and Kenneth P. Langton, *Political Socialization* (New York, 1969), pp. 21-51, and 84-119.
22. See in particular the evidence from Kurt Lewin's pioneering studies of decision-making in small groups which is summarized in R. K. White and Ronald Lippitt, *Autocracy and Democracy* (New York, 1960).
23. William Kornhauser, *The Politics of Mass Society* (London, 1960), pp. 72-73; see also the evidence on the relationship of voluntary group membership and political behaviour in Allan Kornberg, Harold Clarke, and Joel Smith, *Citizen Politicians: Political Socialization and Party Activism in Democratic Society* (Durham, N.C., 1979).
24. Almond and Verba, *The Civic Culture,* p. 294.

25. Excellent summaries of this research can be found in Paul Blumberg, *Industrial Democracy: The Sociology of Participation* (New York, 1973), especially chapters 5 and 6; and Carole Pateman, *Participation and Democratic Theory* (London, 1970), chapters 3-5. On the applicability of this argument to Canada see, H. B. Wilson, *Democracy and the Workplace* (Montreal, 1974).

26. Blumberg, *Industrial Democracy,* p. 123.

27. A. S. Tannenbaum, "Personality Change as a Result of an Experimental Change of Enviromental Conditions", *Journal of Abnormal and Social Psychology,* Vol. 55 (November 1957), pp. 404-06. Support for this proposition in Canada is provided by Mishler, "Political Participation and the Process of Political Socialization in Canada", chapters 4-6.

28. Blumberg, *Industrial Democracy,* p. 109.

29. Harry Eckstein, "A Theory of Stable Democracy", Appendix B in his *Division and Cohesion in Democracy* (Princeton, 1966), p. 229.

30. See, however, the contradictory arguments in Rackman, "A Behavioral Evaluation of the Critique of Behavioralism", paper presented to the Annual Meeting of the American Political Science Association, September 1969.

31. Douglas A. Hibbs, Jr., *Mass Political Violence: A Cross-National Causal Analysis* (New York, 1973), pp. 116-21.

32. Dennis Kavanagh, "Political Behavior and Political Participation", in Geraint Parry, ed., *Participation in Politics* (Manchester, 1972), p. 107.

33. Samuel P. Huntington, *Political Order in Changing Societies* (New Haven, 1968), p. 47. See also Milbrath, *Political Participation,* Chapter 6.

34. Hibbs, *Mass Political Violence,* pp. 96-115.

35. Blumberg, *Industrial Democracy,* chapters 5 and 6; and Almond and Verba, *The Civic Culture,* Chapter 13.

36. Eckstein, *Division and Cohesion in Democracy,* p. 237.

37. See, for example, the very lucid discussion of the problems of maintaining democratic practices and procedures even in small political organizations in Robert A. Dahl and Edward R. Tufte, *Size and Democracy* (Stanford, 1973).

8. The Prospects for Democratic Citizenship

The appeal of democracy is compelling, so much so that even though relatively few nations observe even minimal standards of democratic decision-making, virtually all rely on democratic forms and symbols to establish and sustain legitimacy. Even the most authoritarian regimes pay lip service to democratic ideals, often maintaining that their authoritarian structures are transient and are necessary only until the prerequisites for democracy are established. The principle of citizen participation is a central facet of democracy's appeal—not only in nations such as Canada where the value of the individual is cherished, but also in polities where collectivist values obtain. It is not surprising, therefore, that the concept of participation is a growth stock or that demands for increased citizen participation in virtually all aspects of modern life continue to proliferate.

Ironically, the importance of participation in democratic theory has become the subject of increasing criticism and debate. Where once participation and democracy were virtually synonymous, revisionist theories now frequently view citizen participation as a relatively minor and not altogether desirable characteristic of a stable democratic polity. Indeed, they contend, widespread and intense participation is dangerous in the extreme and is to be avoided. The crux of the contemporary controversy in democratic theory, as has been noted, rests on a series of empirical questions concerning the structure and quality of citizen participation in political life, the causes and consequences of participation and apathy, and the prospects for change. This volume has attempted to clarify the issues in this debate and to probe the literature on political behaviour in

Canada for answers to some of the central questions. In concluding, it is time to review the arguments and evidence and to assess the prospects for democratic citizenship in Canada.

We began this study by noting that classical and contemporary (or elitist) theories of democracy differ in a number of fundamental respects. Distrusting other bases of political authority, classical democrats such as John Stuart Mill relied on widespread citizen participation and the principle of majority rule. Although they realized that relatively few citizens were likely to possess the tolerance, political competence, or rational activist spirit their theories demanded, the classical democrats were convinced these virtues could be encouraged through proper education and, in particular, the provision of significant opportunities for citizen participation in non-political aspects of life. They believed the achievement and maintenance of democratic virtues required constant practice and emphasized the value of participation for promoting individual moral growth and intellectual development. More than a blueprint for the process of governing, therefore, the classical theories were based on a vision of man's democratic potential.

Elitist theories of democracy, in contrast, largely ignore the question of man's democratic potential, focusing instead on current patterns of behaviour. Although advanced as value-free or at least value-neutral, elitist theories nevertheless frequently go beyond description to provide an apology for existing political structures and processes. Observing the widespread apathy, political ignorance, and intolerance characteristic of large segments even of the most advanced and liberal polities, the elitists suggest that apathy and intolerance are probably inevitable and conclude as a consequence that increased citizen participation is as infeasible as it is dangerous. They argue not only that increased participation would tax the capacities of exisiting political institutions but would probably polarize society and jeopardize political stability. Thus, according to one of the better known critics of these views:

> The elitist theories have transformed democracy from a radical to a conservative political doctrine, stripping away its distinctive emphasis on popular political activity so that it no

longer serves as a set of ideals toward which society ought to be striving. . . . The contemporary version of democratic theory has, it seems, lost much of its vital force. . . .[1]

Elitist theories have changed the focus of concern from the individual to society. They have elevated political stability to the level of religion and have enshrined the *status quo* as a formidable, though unattractive god.[2]

In their assumptions regarding participation and man's democratic potential, the classical and elitist theories occupy polar positions in the democratic debate. We have suggested, however, that a reconciliation and synthesis can be achieved in what we have termed the theory of representative democracy. Acknowledging the need for full-time, professional politicians to hold the formal decision-making positions and manage day-to-day affairs in large and complex political systems, representative democracy proposes increased citizen participation in middle-range, though still amateur political activities (such as party work, campaign activity, or community service) that, more than elections, appear to influence both the responsiveness of political leaders and the distribution of societal resources. By providing moderately increased participation in political life, and still greater participation in such non-political spheres as the family, school, and workplace, the theory of representative democracy preserves the classical emphasis on the educational value of participation while responding to the elitists' practical objections concerning the problems of accommodating large numbers of participants who have little appreciation for democratic values. Although clearly based on an optimistic assessment of man's democratic capacity, the representative theory narrows the gap between the vision of the classical democrats and the realities of contemporary behaviour; it establishes less stringent standards of behaviour, and a strengthened program of civic education thereby increasing the prospects for their reconciliation.

Current patterns of political behaviour in Canada generally conform to the elitist model, albeit with important qualifications. Although the structure of political participation in Canada is not as narrow—nor citizen values as authoritarian—as elitist theory suggests, historically, citizen participation has been limited primarily to electoral forms of political activity, to voting in particular. About one-fifth to one-quarter of the eligible population participates in more intensive activities, but an equivalent proportion of the public abstains from politics altogether. Moreover, although the size of the eligible population has increased substantially as many of the formal barriers to participation have been reduced or eliminated, the rate of citizen participation in most activities has remained relatively constant. Consequently, although the apathy and inactivity of Canadian citizens is frequently exaggerated, the contemporary structure of political participation in Canada does resemble the elitist model—a pyramid, broad at the base, tapering sharply through the middle range to a narrow peak.

The evidence regarding the quality of citizen participation in Canada supports a similar conclusion. Consistent with elitist expectations (and classical democratic fears) the average Canadian does not resemble the classical conception of *homo civicus*. Many citizens display little interest in or awareness of politics and political affairs; manifest relatively strong feelings of political cynicism, alienation, and political incompetence; and demonstrate only minimal political rationality according to a strict definition of the term. At the same time, however, very few citizens conform to Freud's notion of *homo homini lupus,* "creatures among whose instinctual endowments is to be reckoned a powerful share of aggressiveness".[3] Though not endowed with a developed sense of tolerance or a democratic ethos, neither is the citizen an aggressive, politically rapacious beast. More persuasive is the image of the citizen as an individual poorly prepared for democratic participation and uncertain of his abilities to cope with the complexities of what seems at times an alien environment.

Although the elitists provide a generally accurate description of the behaviour of an average citizen, they overlook substantial variations and miss the significance of these differences for citizens' democratic potential. The fact that among particular groups of citizens almost half of the eligible population participates in middle-level activities (or would participate if asked) strongly suggests the possibility of establishing a more representative structure of participation by recreating throughout Canada those conditions responsible for higher rates of participation within the most active groups. To take one example, it appears likely, given higher levels of political competition and more effective political-party organizations in Canada, that citizen participation in political campaigns and party activities could be almost doubled even without attempting more fundamental transformations of political structures or institutions. And because citizenship does appear to improve with practice, the quality of participation in Canada seems likely to increase in direct proportion to the expansion of political activity.

The prospects for expanding citizen participation in Canada are further improved by an examination of the psychological and sociological correlates of political activity. Far from being products of man's intrinsic apathy, as elitist theories frequently imply, the relatively low levels of citizen participation in Canada appear to be consequences of complex sets of individual motivations or attitudes whose origins can be traced to a series of individual social and economic experiences associated with the nature of the times in which the individual was reared and the citizen's current position in society. Although individual attitudes and experiences vary widely, a generalized sense of alienation and personal powerlessness bred, at least partly, of the elitist character of Canadian society, the lack of a strong national identity, and the absence of significant opportunities for individual participation in fundamental social, economic, and political institutions underlie and help explain the pervasiveness of political apathy and intolerance in Canada, especially among those on the periphery of society. Francophone Canadians, the poor and poorly educated, the very old and very young, women (though increasingly less so), and those who inhabit Canada's inner cities are but a few of the many groups of citizens with objective reasons for believing themselves to be disadvantaged in society and relatively powerless as individuals to bring about significant change. Reared in undemocratic environments, permitted few opportunities for self-determination even in relatively mundane aspects of their lives, and frequently employed in highly routinized, boring, and subservient positions, the wonder is *not* that many citizens develop personalities inconsistent with classical democratic theory, but that so many overcome these debilitating experiences and become active in the political life of the community at all. Indeed, given that political protest and violence are nourished by feelings of alienation and anomie such as pervade large segments of the Canadian polity, perhaps the real wonder is that non-participation continues to be the norm and has given way to political violence only in isolated instances.

The foundations of political apathy and intolerance, then, are laid early in life and consistently reinforced thereafter. Because, as well, early-life agents of political learning tend to be non-political and are related to the individual by largely non-rational bonds of trust and affection, political attitudes acquired early in life are remarkably resilient and difficult to change. Barring fundamental changes in the structure of the family or the organization and philosophy of education—changes currently beyond the realm of feasible government action—the short-term prospects for engineering wholesale changes in basic personality traits are poor. However, the literature on industrial democracy provides ample evidence that less fundamental, though significant, changes in specific political attitudes could be achieved through relatively modest, non-radical, and cost-effective reforms in industrial authority structures. Even such minor reforms as creating opportunities for worker participation in determining work schedules and developing production quotas could enhance the worker's sense of self-control and self-esteem, increase his tolerance of others and his willingness to defer to the authority of majority rule, and increase his interest and activity in numerous areas of life, including politics. Moreover, by increasing individual satisfaction with work, the likelihood is that the quality and efficiency of worker production would increase apace. Although such modifications would not instantly transform political apathetics into gladiators, they probably would effect marginal, incremental increases in middle-level or transitional activities of the type presupposed by the representative theory. They would increase the size of the active electorate, broaden the base of political-party and interest-group activities, and increase the proportion of citizens willing and able to petition their elected representatives or join in the activities of community action groups in attempts to alter the direction of public policy and make government decisions more responsive. Furthermore, because participation tends to reinforce appropriate attitudes and behaviour, it is reasonable to speculate that the increased political activity produced by enhancing industrial democracy would set in motion a chain reaction leading ultimately to more fundamental changes in political personality and behaviour. Such changes, if they occur, probably would contribute to a political environment in which reforms of educational or even familial authority patterns could be accomplished, thereby enhancing the prospects for approximating the citizenship prerequisites of classical democracy among future generations.

Given that increases in middle-range political activities are feasible, the final question is whether such increases are desirable. Our examination of the consequences of participation suggests, on balance, they are. Viewed strictly from an instrumental perspective, there is some support for the elitists' position that increasing the average rate of citizen participation would little influence the composition of Canada's political leadership or the responsiveness of existing political institutions. Current levels of participation together with the possibility, however remote, that public opinion can be mobilized on specific issues, assure minimal standards of accountability and responsiveness to public interests in the *aggregate*. The instrumental value of increasing participation becomes apparent only when public interests are disaggregated by social and economic status. For obvious reasons, political leaders in Canada traditionally have been most sensitive to the needs and demands of those who are most active in politics. Because this politically active strata is composed disproportionately of the social and economic elite, the interests of disadvantaged segments of Canadian society have suffered by comparison. Consequently, although a general increase in citizen participation would have little impact on public policy, increases specifically in the political activity of the less advantaged in society would foster more equitable representation of all political interests and further strengthen the democratic principle of majority rule.

Even stronger evidence exists of the educational value of participation. We have noted, now, at several points, that higher levels of citizen activity do contribute to the development of more politically mature, psychologically healthy, and socially well-adjusted citizens. This is not to suggest that increased participation, either in politics or in other aspects of society, is necessary or sufficient for the development of democratic personalities. Human behaviour clearly is too complex to be explained by a single variable—even one whose effects are as wide and deep as those of participation. Nevertheless, it is apparent that political activity enhances both the level and sophistication of an individual's political knowledge; it increases the individual's self-esteem and promotes the self-confidence necessary for political tolerance; and it strengthens the individual's support for and commitment to the political community, its institutions, laws, and leaders. Increased participation may even, as Mill contends, contribute to the individual's moral development by enhancing the citizens' ability "to weigh interests not his own; to be guided, in case of conflicting claims, by another rule than his private partialities; to apply, at every turn, principles and maxims which have for their reason of existence the common good."[4]

Finally, increased political participation is of value to society. Contrary to the elitists' view, raising the level of citizen activity in Canada is not likely to exacerbate existing cleavages or rend the fabric of political authority. By providing more equitable representation of all political interests and fostering more democratic personalities, increases in participation seem likely to enhance the legitimacy of existing institutions thereby strengthening political order and stability. However, even were this not the case, there are good reasons for increasing citizen participation in political life. Government structures and institutions are valuable and warrant preservation only insofar as they protect the interests of all citizens and facilitate individual development. Where existing institutions fail in these regards, a certain amount of instability and disorder may be healthy for democracy, elitist assumptions notwithstanding.

Understandably, the proposal to foster self-development by

manipulating individual behaviour may strike some as inconsistent, or worse, as a positive danger to individual freedom. There is widespread reluctance to countenance social engineering or directed social change when applied to human behaviour. The fear seems to be that attempts to encourage specific values or cultivate specific patterns of behaviour are inconsistent with democracy and would hasten the arrival of 1984—the Orwellian spectre of a totalitarian society looms larger as it approaches, no longer a distant vision on the horizon. Even social scientists, for whom social prescription is a stock in trade, "grow faint hearted when questions of [behaviour] control or manipulation are raised. A powerful democratic prejudice dampens their zeal."[5]

Yet, the conception of social science for its own sake devoid of instrumental purpose or policy impact would be rejected by most practitioners. Many social scientists compare their craft to medicine and define its purpose as the search for understanding of the relationship between man and government in order to better diagnose political ills, prescribe appropriate remedies, and thus improve the condition of man's existence. Such a view clearly underlies the literature on Canadian political institutions with its emphasis on political evaluation and reform.

There is a tendency, however, to view individual behaviour as an inappropriate target for these efforts. This ignores the fact that changes in political institutions invariably have human consequences, however unintended or indirect, and assumes, as well, that existing patterns of behaviour are in some way natural, immutable, or products of man's free will. According to Kenneth Langton:

Somehow the "natural" or more accurately the random socialization process has taken on a moral quality of its own. Many think that directed social change smacks of *1984*. However, this stance overlooks the fact that considerable social manipulation, for better or for worse, is taking place anyway.[6]

The evidence presented in this volume suggests that current patterns of behaviour are neither natural nor inevitable. Nor are they entirely the products of individual volition. At least part of human behaviour is learned and the individual has little control over either the content or process of education.

In a sense, then, the concern over the propriety of social engineering is misplaced. The important question to be confronted is not whether man's behaviour should be controlled; some degree of control is present and inevitable. The important question, rather, is whether behaviour will be regulated openly and rationally with ample opportunity for the discussion of alternatives and consequences or be allowed to continue in a largely random non-rational fashion guided for the most part by tradition—the reasons for which (if there ever were reasons) have long been forgotten—with few opportunities for analysis and possible improvement. The *a priori* rejection of social engineering as an alternative only impedes the discussion of values, the danger of which is clearly diagnosed by David Easton:

> . . . By failing to encourage within the discipline creative speculation about political alternatives in the broadest sense, we cannot help but imprison ourselves within the limitations of the ongoing value framework. . . . Knowledge brings an awareness of alternatives and their consequences . . . [and] imposes special obligations on the knower. . . . it is therefore immoral for him not to act.[7]

There is no doubt that social engineering is open to abuse or that the attendant dangers are severe. But there are comparable risks in any alternative—not the least of which includes the perpetuation of the status quo. By refusing to accept responsibility for the direction of society, we abandon choice for chance and acquiesce in the widespread alienation and apathy that deprive so many citizens of human dignity and self-respect.

The weight of the evidence presented in this volume strongly supports elitist theory as a description of current patterns of political participation in Canada, but suggests that a closer approximation of the classical democratic model is both feasible and desirable. It is unrealistic to advocate the direct participation of all citizens in every decision with significant consequences for their lives; obvious limits on the number of individuals who can sit in parliament, hold administrative positions in government, or formally express an opinion on specific legislation make inevitable our reliance on a set of political institutions in which a relatively few individuals make decisions for the many. But having conceded the necessity for full-time political professionals to represent the public at the highest levels of the political process, there remain substantial opportunities for expanding citizen participation in middle-range political activities thereby achieving a more representative democracy in which citizens can more fully realize their individual potentials and achieve larger measures of self-esteem, personal satisfaction, and psychological well being. Only by trusting our collective wisdom and seizing the opportunity to expand participation can we create the conditions necessary for a more representative government and realize, at least, the promise of democracy.

NOTES

1. Jack Walker, "A Critique of the Elitist Theory of Democracy", *American Political Science Review,* Vol. 60 (June 1966), p. 288.
2. Lewis Lipsitz, "Vulture, Mantis, and Seal: Proposals for Political Scientists," *Polity,* Vol. 3 (September 1970), pp. 3-21.
3. Sigmund Freud, *Civilization and Its Discontents,* trans. by James Strachey (New York, 1961), p. 58.
4. "Considerations on Representative Government", p. 291.
5. James Steintranger, "Political Socialization and Political Theory", *Social Research,* Vol. 35 (Spring 1968), p. 121.
6. Kenneth Langton, *Political Socialization* (New York, 1969), p. 175.
7. David Easton, "The New Revolution in Political Science", *American Political Science Review,* Vol. 63 (December 1969), pp. 1058-59.

Index